BUON **NATALE**

JOYEUX **NOEL**

MERRY **CHRISTMAS**

FELIZ **NAVIDAD**

MELE **KALIKIMAKA**

VROLIJK **KERSTFEEST**

GOD **JUL**

MERI **KURISUMASU**

FROHE **WEIHNACHTEN**

NOLLIG **SHONA**

HAVE A VERY MERRY

TOLE-PAINTED
CHRISTMAS

HAVE A VERY MERRY
TOLE-PAINTED
CHRISTMAS

KRISTEN BIRKELAND, CDA &
HEIDI FASSMANN, CDA

Sterling Publishing Co., Inc.
New York
A Sterling / Chapelle Book

Chapelle:

Owner: Jo Packham

Editor: Cathy Sexton

Staff: Areta Bingham, Kass Burchett, Ray Cornia, Marilyn Goff, Karla Haberstich, Holly Hollingsworth, Susan Jorgensen, Barbara Milburn, Karmen Quinney, Caroll Shreeve, Cindy Stoeckl, Kim Taylor, Sara Toliver, Desirée Wybrow

Photography: Kevin Dilley for Hazen Imaging, Inc.
Photo Stylist: Jill Dahlberg

If you have any questions or comments or would like information on specialty products featured in this book, please contact: Chapelle, Ltd., Inc. P.O. Box 9252, Ogden, UT 84409 (801) 621-2777 • (801) 621-2788 Fax • e-mail: chapelle@chapelleltd.com • web site: www.chapelleltd.com

The projects in this book were created for the intermediate/advanced painter. Previous painting experience is highly recommended. The written instructions, projects, diagrams, patterns, illustrations, and photographs in this volume are intended for the personal use of the reader. Any other use, especially commercial use, is forbidden under law without the written permission of the copyright holder. Every effort has been made to ensure that all the information in this book is accurate. However, due to differing conditions, tools, and individual skills, the publisher cannot be responsible for any injuries, losses, and/or other damages which may result from the use of the information in this book. Due to the limited amount of space available, we must print our patterns at a reduced size in order to give our patrons the maximum number of patterns possible in our publications. We believe the quality and quantity of our patterns will compensate for any inconvenience this may cause.

The instructions for the Rosemal Sled shown on page 122 have not been included in this publication. Contact Chapelle, Ltd., Inc. for this information.

Library of Congress Cataloging-in-Publication Data Available

10 9 8 7 6 5 4 3 2 1

Published by Sterling Publishing Co., Inc.
387 Park Avenue South, New York, NY 10016
© 2002 by Chapelle Ltd.
Distributed in Canada by Sterling Publishing
c/o Canadian Manda Group, One Atlantic Avenue, Suite 105
Toronto, Ontario, Canada M6K 3E7
Distributed in Great Britain and Europe by Chrysalis Books
64 Brewery Road, London N7 9NT, England
Distributed in Australia by Capricorn Link (Australia) Pty. Ltd.
P.O. Box 704, Windsor, NSW 2756, Australia
Printed in China
All Rights Reserved

Sterling ISBN 0-8069-7651-9

TABLE OF CONTENTS

INTRODUCTION

What better way to create lasting heirlooms than through decorative painting. Hand-painted items are wonderful for home decorating anytime of the year, but Christmas is a particularly exciting time of year for decorating. From the traditional Santa Claus to tiny ornaments to large trunks, your home can be filled with one-of-a-kind treasures that brighten every corner of every room. Painting on functional pieces, such as furniture, dishes, and toys, also makes cheery additions to Christmas decorating.

Everyone has certain Christmas decorations that immediately send them on a nostalgic trip to years past. Treasures made by youthful hands and gifts from people near and dear. Some decorations will remind you of a special trip, a school friend, or your favorite grandmother.

Kristen and Heidi, both Certified Decorative Artists with the Society of Decorative Painters, have 43 years of combined painting experience. Kristen's Norwegian background and Heidi's German heritage have been a significant influence throughout both painting careers. The special interest each has in the native folk art of their ancestors has helped them explore decorative painting in all its forms.

Their hope is that every painter will find projects in this book that will inspire, challenge, teach, and help bring satisfaction and joy to everyone who paints and to everyone who receives beautiful hand-painted pieces from someone they love.

Supplies You Will Need To Have On Hand:

- Acrylic Paints
- Brush Basin
- Chalk Pencil or
  Soapstone Pencil
- Cloths
- Flow Medium
- Glazing Medium
- Hot-glue Gun
- Liquid Soap
- Metal Primer
- Mop
- Paintbrushes
- Paper Towels
- Pencils
- Polyurethane
  Water-based Varnish
- Retarder or Extender
- Rubbing Alcohol
- Sandpaper
- Sponges
- Spray Varnish
- Stylus
- Tack Cloth
- Tracing Paper
- Transfer Paper or
  Graphite Paper
- Transparent Tape
- Vinegar
- Waxed Palette
- Wood Glue
- Wood Putty
- Wood Sealer

Paintbrushes:

Almost any brand of paint-brush is good when it is new. The most important thing is that it needs to be clean and well shaped. When paint begins to build up inside the ferrule, the paintbrush will no longer perform the way it was intended.

For most acrylic painting, synthetic paintbrushes are best, but there are certain techniques where a natural-bristled paintbrush is more suitable.

A paintbrush should have enough "snap" to it to return to its original shape after painting a stroke. Paint-brushes that are too soft and lack body make painting difficult.

Your greatest investment as a painter will be in quality paintbrushes. You will need a variety of styles and sizes. A good set of brushes should include, but not be limited to:

- Sizes 4, 8, 12, 14 Flats
- Sizes 2, 4 Liners
- Sizes 0, 2, 4 Rounds
- Sizes 0, 1, 10/0 Script Liners
- Sizes 4, 6, 8 Filberts
- Sizes $3/4$", 1" Flat Wash(s)
- Sizes $1/4$", $1/2$" Rakes (Tooth)
- Size 3 Quill (Raphael Kolinsky®)

In addition, there are a number of "specialty" paint-brushes available that have specific purposes. These may include a Rake (Tooth or Comb), Fan, Deerfoot, and Dagger.

It is good to have a supply of old worn-out paintbrushes on hand also.

Paintbrush Care:

Most commercial brush basins were designed with at least three compartments. One or two for cleaning— they have teeth on the bottom for gently forcing the paint out of the paintbrush. The other compartment is for rinsing.

If you will always wash and rinse your paintbrush before you set it down, you will be able to walk away from your painting at any time and know that your paintbrushes are not being ruined by dry paint.

Every so often it is a good idea to give your paint-brushes a bit of extra care. Clean them with liquid soap, pinch out excess water, and let them air dry. It is best to let them dry lying down so that water does not soak into

the handle through the ferrule. Once dry, it is recommended that paintbrushes be stored upright in a container.

Rubbing alcohol can remove paint from a totally neglected paintbrush, but it cannot restore its shape. Once a paintbrush loses its chisel or point, do yourself a favor and get a new brush—you will be glad you did!

Wood Preparation:

The majority of the projects in this book are painted on wooden surfaces. Check for holes, cracks, and other imperfections in the surface. If necessary, fill with wood putty. In any case, sand until smooth. Wipe with a tack cloth to remove dust. Apply one coat of wood sealer, following manufacturer's directions, and let dry. Don't neglect to seal your wood as it will make a big difference in your painting. Floating, linework, and strokework will be much easier to do if you have properly prepared your painting surface. When the sealer is dry, lightly sand with a superfine sandpaper. Again wipe with a tack cloth to remove dust. Remember—sand, seal, sand.

Galvanized Metal Preparation:

Galvanized metal has an oily film that must be removed before painting. Using a moistened cloth, wash the metal surface with a mixture of vinegar and water (1:1), but do not immerse the piece in water. To roughen the surface, lightly sand with a superfine sandpaper. Wipe with a tack cloth to remove dust. Spray the piece with several light coats of metal primer, following manufacturer's directions, and let dry for 24 hours before proceeding.

Transferring Patterns:

Begin by tracing or copying your design onto a piece of tracing paper—something that you can see through. Sometimes this can be a bit tedious, but it is important to be able to see through your paper so that you can accurately place it on your painting surface. Tracing will also help familiarize you with the design before you begin to paint.

After placing the pattern over the surface, slide a piece of transfer or graphite paper between the design and the surface. Using a stylus, trace the design again. Transfer only the main elements of the design—do not transfer details that will be covered up by base-coating.

Sometimes pieces are oddly shaped and sculpted. Applying a traced pattern with transfer or graphite paper is nearly impossible and is rarely done accurately. The best way to apply a guide for painting is to draw it on with a chalk or soapstone pencil. Refer to the photographs provided for placement and don't be afraid to go back and rebase an area to get it the way you want it. Keep in mind that "different" isn't "wrong." Make adjustments to suit your own taste.

You are now ready to begin painting. Following is a list of painting terms along with a brief description of each for your reference.

Working with Acrylic Paints:

Begin by squeezing a "puddle" of paint about the size of a nickel onto your palette. Using a paintbrush, pull the paint from the edge of the puddle. Avoid dipping the paintbrush in the center of the puddle.

Let each coat of paint dry before applying another coat.

Base-coating:

Base-coating is simply covering an entire area with one initial color of acrylic paint until the surface is opaque. Paint must be smooth, without ridges or brush strokes. Starting in the center and painting toward the outer edges will prevent ridges on the edges. Light coats are better than heavy coats. For better coverage, apply several light coats as necessary.

Floating:

Floating, or side-loading, is an imperative technique to master in order to create soft shadows and highlights. Ninety-nine percent of the time you should float with a size 12 or larger flat paintbrush. Even tiny eyes can be floated with a large brush if it is loaded correctly.

Most of the shading and highlighting on the projects in this book are done with floating. The paintbrush is dipped in clean water, then blotted on a paper towel until the "shine" disappears. Be careful not to remove all the water from the bristles as there is a certain amount of water needed in order to create a softly blended stroke. Dip the corner of the paintbrush into some fresh paint. Begin blending both sides of the paintbrush on your palette. When properly blended, the paintbrush should have paint on one side and clean water on the other. Paint should never reach the water side of the paintbrush. If it does, rinse the paintbrush and start over.

Whenever possible, begin the floating strokes away from you and draw it toward you instead of painting sideways or backhanded. Set the flat surface of the paintbrush down and give it some pressure—you want to "squeeze" the paint and water out of the paintbrush as you apply the stroke. Practice on mat board or cardboard that has been based with several coats of acrylic paint. Do not use paper as paper soaks the water out of the brush and makes floating impossible.

Several strokes, such as "S" strokes and "C" strokes, are created with floating. These strokes simply resemble the appropriate letters.

Washing:

Applying a wash onto a surface will allow a very thin, transparent coat of paint to cover the surface. When washing, create a mixture of up to 80% water to 20% paint. It is especially important to let each application dry before applying subsequent layers.

Dry-brushing:

Dry-brushing is used for adding shading and highlighting to certain areas of a design. Load a dry paintbrush with an appropriate value of paint, then wipe most of the paint from the paintbrush onto a dry paper towel. Dry-brush onto the surface by gently "scrubbing" the area. Be patient and let the color build up gradually.

When dry-brushing cheeks, remove all of the paint from the paintbrush, leaving only a small amount of pigment in the bristles. Gently "scrub" in a circular motion until you achieve the desired brightness.

You can dry-brush small, thin areas such as stems and vines with a small liner brush. The paint does not need to be as dry as in the previous method, but the paintbrush should not be overloaded. Wipe some of the paint out of the paintbrush before applying it to the surface. Stroke the paint repeatedly in the small areas, "coaxing" the paint from the paintbrush.

Stippling:

Stippling is used to render a textured look to a specific element of a design such as fur, trees, and grass. It is done by "pouncing" in an up-and-down motion on the surface with a paintbrush specifically designed for this purpose, or with an old worn-out paintbrush that no longer holds a chisel edge.

Depending on the effect desired, stippling can be done with a heavy application of paint or with a light application of paint.

Double-loading:

Using an appropriately sized flat paintbrush for the project you are painting, fully load the paintbrush in the medium value of paint, then pick up a small amount of the light or dark value on the corner of the paintbrush. Blend both sides of the brush on your palette, blending the colors together to create two values on the same paintbrush. Blending is very important, allowing a transition in value—you do not want a sharp line in the center.

Reverse Teardrops:

Reverse teardrops are a traditional stroke used extensively in rosemaling, but they are also used in other forms of folk art. The best paintbrush that I have found for perfecting these strokes is the Raphael Kolinsky Quill #3.

Load the paintbrush with fresh paint. Holding the paintbrush with the handle upward, lightly set the tip of the paintbrush down and begin to drag as you increase pressure on the paintbrush. End the stroke by setting the belly of the paintbrush down, creating the fat, rounded end of the stroke. Lift the brush straight up.

Double-loaded reverse teardrops are executed in the same way; however, they have two values of paint in the paintbrush. Load the paintbrush in the light value, then tip in the dark value.

Linework:

Linework can make or ruin a beautiful painting project. Learning to do nice linework takes practice, but is well worth the effort.

Linework is best done with a long-bristled paintbrush—a scroller or script liner. Paint should be slightly thinner than when it comes from the bottle. Flow Medium or water can be added, but the end result should be an "inky" consistency. Load the paintbrush, then drag it through the paint and roll the tip into a fine point. Hold your paintbrush handle upward, dragging it along the pattern line. If necessary, use your little finger as a brace.

Finishing:

There are a number of ways to finish a project. For special heirloom pieces, items that are intended for use, or pieces that may get handled repeatedly, it is recommended that from three or four coats to as many as ten coats of polyurethane water-based varnish, matte or satin, be applied.

In this book there are many projects that are difficult to finish with a brush-on varnish. In these instances, a spray varnish can be used to seal the pieces. Several light coats are recommended.

When using a spray varnish, make certain to remove all pattern lines before varnishing. Also remember to varnish your project before gluing on embellishments such as hair, clothing, and other accessories.

14

THE NATIVITY

Paint Palette:

Delta:
Black
Black Green
Blue Spruce
Burnt Sienna
Burnt Umber
Chamomile
Charcoal
Dark Brown
Dark Burnt Umber
Drizzle Grey
Flesh: Dark, Medium
Flesh Tan
Ivory
Leprechaun
Light Ivory
Maple Sugar
Mudstone
Palomino
Pine Green
Quaker Grey
Rain Grey
Raw Sienna
Rouge
Sandstone
Spice Brown
Spice Tan
Storm Grey
Terra Cotta
Territorial Beige
Trail
Victorian Teal:
    Dark, Light, Medium
Wedgewood Green
White

Supplies:
Wooden Nativity
    with Manger

All Faces and Hands:

1. Base faces, necks, hands, and wrists with Medium Flesh. Shade with Dark Flesh.

2. Blush cheeks and noses with Rouge.

3. Line eyes with Black and mouths with Dark Flesh + Rouge. Line eyebrows with Burnt Umber.

4. Line some hair across foreheads (except on Baby Jesus) with shades of Dark Brown, Burnt Umber, and Dark Burnt Umber.

Shepherd:

Note: Using a chalk pencil, draw robes and drapes on figures. After basing, add folds and wrinkles on appropriate articles of clothing.

1. Base gown with Trail. Shade with Territorial Beige, then again with Dark Brown. Highlight neckline with Trail + Light Ivory.

2. Base one small and one large stripe around bottom of gown with Burnt Sienna. Dry-brush through center of large stripe with Terra Cotta. Base stripes on sleeves and neck with Burnt Sienna.

3. Base belt with Dark Brown.

4. Base drape with Flesh Tan. Shade with Palomino. Highlight with Ivory.

5. Base headdress with Spice Brown.

6. Base stripes on headdress with Burnt Umber + Glazing Medium. Dry-brush highlight between stripes with Territorial Beige.

7. Base headband with Burnt Sienna. Dry-brush lines with Terra Cotta. Shade next to headband with Dark Burnt Umber.

Mary:

1. Base gown with Sandstone. Stipple with Sandstone + Light Ivory, then again with Light Ivory. Shade with Mudstone, then again with Mudstone + a small amount of Dark Burnt Umber.

2. Base robe and headdress with Dark Victorian Teal. Highlight robe with Medium Victorian Teal, then again with Light Victorian Teal. Shade with Blue Spruce, then again with Blue Spruce + Black Green.

3. Base both stripes along bottoms of headdress and headband with Chamomile. Shade with Spice Tan. Highlight with Light Ivory.

4. Base belt and trim along edge of robe with Blue Spruce. Shade with Blue Spruce + Black Green. Highlight with Medium Victorian Teal.

Joseph:

1. Base gown with Quaker Grey. Stipple with Quaker Grey + White. Shade with Rain Grey, then again with Storm Grey.

2. Base robe with Pine Green. Highlight with Leprechaun, then again with Wedgewood Green. Shade with Black Green.

3. Base stripe near bottom of robe with Spice Tan. Shade with Raw Sienna. Highlight with Maple Sugar.

4. Base belt with Spice Tan. Add tiny "S" strokes with Burnt Sienna. Highlight between strokes with Maple Sugar.

5. Base headdress with Rain Grey. Highlight with Quaker Grey, then again with Drizzle Grey.

6. Base stripes on headdress with Rain Grey + Storm Grey + Glazing Medium 2:1:1. Shade with Charcoal. Stipple one stripe on headdress with Pine Green.

7. Base headband with Charcoal. Add "S" strokes with Drizzle Grey + Pine Green. Highlight with Drizzle Grey + Pine Green + White.

Baby Jesus:

1. Wash over hair area with a Dark Brown wash. Line some curls on hair with Dark Brown + Burnt Umber. Darken with Dark Burnt Umber.

2. Base body with Light Ivory. Shade with Mudstone. Highlight with White.

Note: If desired, Baby Jesus can be wrapped in a small piece of fabric or felt.

Manger:

1. Lightly wash manger with Spice Brown so woodgrain shows through. Shade with Burnt Umber.

2. To create three wood planks on sides of manger, shade with Dark Burnt Umber. Dry-brush through centers with Raw Sienna.

3. To create nails, apply dots on corner supports with Burnt Umber.

16

Paint Palettes:

Delta:

Apple Green
Black Cherry
Black Green
Chocolate Cherry
Forest Green
Raspberry
Seminole
White

Gleams:

Pearl Finish

Supplies:

Wooden Ornaments (4)
Circle Template

Note: Ornaments must be glued together prior to painting.

Dividing An Ornament into Sections:
Turn ornament so you are looking directly down on the top. Using a chalk pencil, evenly divide the top into fourths. You can then further divide into eighths or twelfths. Use these marks as reference points to create the designs.

©2001 Kristen Birkeland, CDA

4. Base broken stripe around center with Forest Green. Shade with Forest Green + Black Green. Reverse-float highlight with Apple Green.

5. Add descending dots between each stroke at top and bottom with Black Cherry. Highlight dots at top with a small amount of Raspberry.

6. Transfer Holly Pattern from below around ornament.

7. Base holly leaves with Forest Green. Shade leaves and veins with Forest Green + Black Green. Highlight with Apple Green. Dot berries with Black Cherry. Highlight with Raspberry.

8. Add scrolls with Forest Green. Highlight with Apple Green.

9. Add double-loaded reverse teardrops above and below scrolls loaded with Apple Green and tipped with Forest Green. Add descending dots above and below scrolls with Raspberry.

10. For design connecting lower one-strokes, add a large dot above and between tops of one-strokes with Black Cherry. Highlight with a small amount of Raspberry. Add descending dots to encompass large dots with Raspberry. Add an "S" stroke on sides of each large dot with Black Cherry.

11. Add double-loaded reverse teardrops on sides of each large dot loaded with Apple Green and tipped with Forest Green. Add double-loaded reverse teardrops below each large dot loaded with Raspberry and tipped with Black Cherry.

Ornament #1:

1. Base ornament with White, then again with two or three coats of Pearl Finish. Divide into eighths.

2. Base cap with Black Cherry. Base stripe around center of cap with Raspberry.

3. Add one-strokes around top and bottom with Forest Green. Highlight "tips" with Apple Green. Dry-brush "tails" with Forest Green + Black Green.

Holly Pattern

18

Ornament #2:

1. Base ornament with White, then again with two or three coats of Pearl Finish. Divide into twelfths.

2. Base cap with Black Cherry.

3. Add elongated strokes around top with Forest Green. Dry-brush with Apple Green.

4. Add one-strokes in between elongated strokes with Black Cherry.

5. Add a large dot next to bottoms of elongated strokes with Forest Green. Add double-loaded reverse teardrops loaded with Raspberry and tipped with Black Cherry.

6. Base stripe around center with Black Cherry.

7. Add descending dots on stripe with Pearl Finish.

8. Line "C" strokes below stripe with Forest Green. Add a large dot where each "C" connects with Raspberry.

9. Add double-loaded reverse teardrops below each large dot loaded with Raspberry and tipped with Black Cherry.

10. Add one-strokes around bottom with Black Cherry.

Ornament #3:

1. Base ornament and cap with Forest Green. Divide into eighths.

2. Draw a ring around top approximately ⁵/₈" down so all strokes end up the same length.

Note: This can be easily done by placing a circle template over ornament and drawing a circle with a chalk pencil.

3. Add spiraled strokes around top with Seminole. Shade behind right side of each stroke with Forest Green + Black Green. Dry-brush center of each stroke with Apple Green. Line top of each stroke with Forest Green + Black Green.

4. For design connecting upper spiraled strokes, add a large dot at bottom of each spiraled stroke with Black Cherry. Highlight with a small amount of Raspberry.

5. Add one-strokes with Pearl Finish.

6. Transfer Holly Pattern from below around ornament.

7. Base holly leaves with Forest Green. Shade behind tops of leaves with Forest Green + Black Green. Highlight bottom edges of leaves with Apple Green. Dot berries with Black Cherry. Highlight with Raspberry.

8. Add scrolls and veins with Apple Green.

9. Add one-strokes below scrolls with Pearl Finish.

10. Add descending dots around ornament with Black Cherry. Add lines with Seminole. Highlight centers with Apple Green.

11. Add one-strokes around bottom with Pearl Finish.

Holly Pattern

20

Ornament #4:

1. Base ornament and cap with Black Cherry. Divide into eighths.

2. Add double-loaded one-strokes around top loaded with Raspberry and tipped with Pearl Finish.

3. Transfer Holly Pattern from below around ornament.

4. Base holly leaves with Forest Green. Shade behind tops of leaves with Chocolate Cherry. Line upper edges of leaves with Pearl Finish. Highlight bottom edges of leaves with Apple Green.

5. Add scrolls and veins with Apple Green.

6. Add dots with Raspberry. Add one-strokes above and below scrolls with Pearl Finish.

7. Add lines around center with Raspberry. Add descending dots at tops of lines with Pearl Finish.

8. Add scrolls with Forest Green. Dry-brush centers of scrolls with Apple Green. Add a dot at end of each scroll with Seminole. Highlight with a small amount of Apple Green. Add double-loaded one-strokes below scrolls loaded with Raspberry and tipped with Pearl Finish.

9. Add one-strokes around bottom with Pearl Finish.

Holly Pattern

CHRISTMASTIME CLOCK

Paint Palette:

Delta:

Bittersweet
Black
Black Green
Burnt Umber
Cadet Blue
Chocolate Cherry
Deep River
Empire Gold
Green Sea
Leaf Green
Light Ivory
Maple Sugar
Medium Flesh
Metallic Gold
Napthol Crimson
Raw Sienna
Spice Brown
Spice Tan
Tomato Spice
White

Supplies:

Wooden Clock
Old Masters®
    Finishing Stain,
    Early American

*Note: Stain wood
prior to painting.*

Clock:

1. Base roof with Deep River.

2. Transfer shadow box sections from Clock Pattern on page 27 onto clock. Do not add detailing.

Note: The frames around each window section are ¹/₄" wide. Use ¹/₄"-wide tape to mask frames.

3. Shade around outside of outer frame with Burnt Umber as indicated by short vertical lines.

Note: Make certain you are clear on which side of line to float. Each section has a roof and a floor—do not shade along floor line next to green frame. The floor line and vertical wall line are about 1" from frame.

4. Shade under roof with Burnt Umber.

5. Remove tape and base frames with Deep River. Shade frames with Black Green as indicated by short vertical lines. Reverse-float highlight in center of each section with Green Sea, as indicated by xxx's, then again with Green Sea + White.

6. Transfer Clock Pattern onto clock.

Wreath:

1. Shade behind wreath where it will be against frame on left side with Black Green.

2. Stipple with Deep River, then again with Green Sea, then again with Green Sea + White.

3. Base bow with Tomato Spice. Shade with Chocolate Cherry. Highlight with Napthol Crimson. Line edges with Metallic Gold.

4. Line cord with Burnt Umber.

5. Add tiny dots on top with Metallic Gold.

6. Base nail with Black + White. Shade with Black. Highlight with White. Base nail shadow on right with Black.

7. Add some berries with Tomato Spice and some with White.

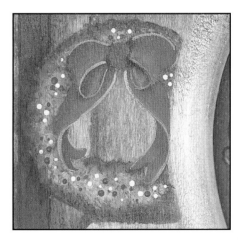

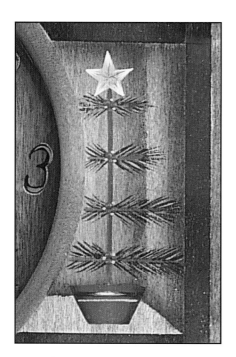

Feather Tree:

1. Line trunk and branches with Burnt Umber. Line needles with Deep River, then again with Green Sea. Line a few needles near trunk with Black Green.

2. Base star with Empire Gold. Highlight tips with Empire Gold + White. Pull tiny lines from center with Metallic Gold.

3. Base pot with Tomato Spice. Shade sides with Chocolate Cherry. Reverse-float a highlight in center with Napthol Crimson.

4. Base a stripe with Deep River. Highlight center of stripe with Green Sea. Base another stripe with Metallic Gold.

5. Dot some berries with Metallic Gold and some with Tomato Spice. Highlight red berries with Napthol Crimson.

Santa:

1. Base hat and suit with Tomato Spice. Shade with Chocolate Cherry. Highlight with Napthol Crimson.

2. Base face with Medium Flesh. Float cheeks and nose with Medium Flesh + Tomato Spice. Add eyes with Black. Line eyebrows with White.

3. Base beard with Black + White. Float "C" strokes with White. Float moustache with White.

4. Base gloves with Deep River. Highlight with Green Sea. Shade with Black Green.

5. Base boots with Black. Highlight with Black + White 1:2.

6. Base fur with Cadet Blue. Stipple with White.

7. Base blocks with White. Add letters with Deep River. Highlight with Green Sea. Line each block and add string with Metallic Gold.

Teddy Bear:

1. Base teddy bear with Spice Tan. Shade with Spice Brown. Stipple with Maple Sugar, then again with Maple Sugar + Light Ivory, then again with Light Ivory on tips of ears, toes, hands, and forehead.

2. Add a stick and string with Spice Brown. Highlight with Empire Gold.

3. Base bell with Raw Sienna. Shade with Chocolate Cherry. Highlight with Empire Gold, then again with Empire Gold + White. Add holes with Chocolate Cherry.

4. Paint bow as in Wreath, Step 3 on page 23.

5. Add nose with Burnt Umber. Add eye with Black.

Note: If necessary to reinforce shading, float with Spice Brown.

Box:

1. Base box with Tomato Spice. Shade with Chocolate Cherry. Highlight with Napthol Crimson. Line with Metallic Gold.

2. Base bow with Deep River. Shade with Black Green. Highlight with Green Sea.

Stocking:

1. Base stocking with Tomato Spice. Shade with Chocolate Cherry. Highlight with Napthol Crimson.

2. Base toe and heel with White. Line with Metallic Gold. Wash a shadow on toe and heel with Cadet Blue.

3. Base candy cane with White. Add some stripes with Tomato Spice and some with Leaf Green. Wash edges of candy cane with Cadet Blue. To create "shine," add a line with White.

4. Paint nail as in Wreath, Step 6 on page 23.

5. Shade behind stocking on frame with Deep River.

Candle:

1. Dry-brush an area behind where flame will be with Metallic Gold.

2. Base flame with Empire Gold. Shade at base of flame with Tomato Spice. Highlight tip with White.

3. Base candle with Light Ivory. Shade with Raw Sienna. Add drips with White. Shade a tiny bit at bottom edges of drips with Raw Sienna.

4. Base candlestick with Raw Sienna. Shade with Raw Sienna + Chocolate Cherry. Highlight with Maple Sugar, then again with Maple Sugar + Light Ivory.

NOEL Blocks:

1. Base two blocks with Tomato Spice. Shade with Chocolate Cherry. Highlight with Napthol Crimson. Line with White.

2. Base remaining two blocks with White. Wash with Cadet Blue. Line with Tomato Spice.

3. Add letters with Deep River. Highlight with Green Sea, then again with Green Sea + White.

4. Base wagon with Deep River. Shade with Black Green. Highlight with Green Sea, then again with Green Sea + White.

5. Line string with Spice Brown. Add a large dot at end with Tomato Spice. Highlight with a small amount of White.

6. Paint wheels with Tomato Spice. Highlight with Napthol Crimson. Add a dot on each wheel with Metallic Gold.

Basket:

1. Base basket with Spice Brown. Shade with Burnt Umber. Dry-brush weaving and add "S" strokes around rim with Raw Sienna. Highlight "S" strokes and center of weaving area with Maple Sugar. Line one side of "S" strokes with Metallic Gold. Line vertical spines with Burnt Umber.

2. Base apples with Tomato Spice. Shade with Chocolate Cherry. Highlight with Napthol Crimson.

3. Add stems with Burnt Umber.

4. Base oranges with Bittersweet. Lightly stipple with Bittersweet + White to give an "orange peel" texture. Add a stronger highlight in upper right with Bittersweet + a little more White. Shade with Bittersweet + Tomato Spice.

5. Paint peppermint sticks as with candy cane in Stocking, Step 3 on page 25.

Note: For holly leaves in basket, see Holly below.

Presents:

1. Randomly base some presents with Tomato Spice, some with Deep River, and some with White. Shade and highlight Tomato Spice and Deep River presents as in Box, Step 1 on page 25. Shade White presents with a Deep River wash.

2. Paint bows as in Wreath, Step 3 on page 23—some presents do not have bows.

Holly:

1. Base holly leaves and stems with Deep River. Shade each leaf with Black Green. Highlight leaf tips and stems with Green Sea, then again with Green Sea + White.

2. Line one side of each leaf and vein with Metallic Gold.

3. Add some berries with Tomato Spice and some with White.

Clock Face:

1. Make certain opening for clock matches pattern. Adjust as necessary.

2. Shade inside circle with Burnt Umber.

3. Base numbers with Deep River. Dry-brush highlight with Green Sea, then again with Green Sea + White.

4. Line left side of each number with Metallic Gold.

Note: If you are buying clockworks, make certain to buy one with the shortest shaft possible that will still come through thickness of clock face.

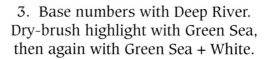

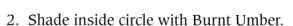

Clock Pattern
Enlarge 111%

Paint Palettes:

Deco Art:
Asphaltum
Black Green
Black Plum
Blue Mist
Bright Green
Burnt Sienna
Dark Pine
Flesh Tone
Graphite
Lamp Black
Marigold
Midnight Blue
Mississippi Mud
Moon Yellow
Neutral Grey
Santa Red
Titanium White

Delta:
Liberty Blue

JoSonja:
Pearl White
Rich Gold

Supplies:

Galvanized Metal Bucket

Note: Seal bucket and let dry overnight prior to painting.

Note: All shading and highlighting floats should be kept "washy" and "layered" for greater color intensity.

Bucket:

1. Base front of bucket with Liberty Blue. Brush diagonally in one direction across bucket leaving it streaky and uneven around edges.

2. Transfer Tree Pattern below, Santa and Bag Pattern on page 32, and Snowman Pattern on page 35 onto bucket.

Trees:

1. Base trunks with Asphaltum. Line with Mississippi Mud. Shade with Black Green.

2. Lay Black Green into triangular corners of trees.

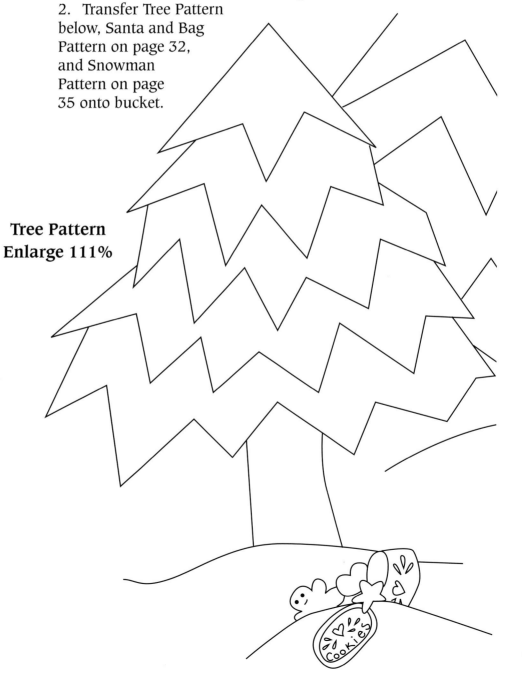

**Tree Pattern
Enlarge 111%**

3. Rake Dark Pine up into Black Green areas, then again with Blue Mist, then again with Titanium White, getting closer to tips with each layer.

4. Glaze over back trees with Liberty Blue. Glaze over front tree with Blue Mist to settle into background.

Snow:

1. Begin stippling snow and snowman with Blue Mist, then again with Blue Mist + Titanium White. Continue stippling adding Titanium White until you are using straight Titanium White.

Note: With each lighter layer, keep lights to top snow ridges and center of snowman.

Santa:

1. Base pants and hat with Santa Red. Apply a thin layer of Retarder over areas, then base with Black Plum. Using a crumpled piece of plastic wrap, pounce over areas. Let dry. Highlight with Moon Yellow + Red. Shade with Black Plum.

2. Stipple fur with Neutral Grey, then again with Neutral Grey + Titanium White, then more Titanium White in center of fur. Shade with Graphite.

3. Base boots and belt with Lamp Black. Dry-brush highlight with Lamp Black + Tita-

nium White. Base belt buckle with Rich Gold. Highlight with Moon Yellow.

4. Base mittens with Black Green. Stipple with Dark Pine, then again with Bright Green.

5. Base face with Flesh Tone. Shade with Burnt Sienna. Darken shadows with Burnt Sienna + Lamp Black. Dry-brush cheeks with Santa Red + Flesh Tone. Highlight with Titanium White.

6. Base eyes with Titanium White. Add irises with Liberty Blue. Add pupils with Lamp Black. Float across tops of eyes with Black. Add a sparkle to eyes with Titanium White. Line eyebrows with Graphite + Titanium White. Lighten with Titanium White.

7. Base beard with Graphite + Titanium White, adding more Titanium White with each layer. Rake in hair. Shade with Graphite.

Bag:

1. Base bag, cord, and tassels with Dark Pine. Shade with Black Green. Dry-brush highlight with Bright Green.

2. Line tassels with Rich Gold.

Ball:

1. Base ball with Liberty Blue.

2. Add design on ball with Titanium White.

3. Shade with Midnight Blue. Highlight with Titanium White.

Present:

1. Base present in Santa Red. Highlight with Santa Red + Moon Yellow. Shade with Black Plum.

2. Base ribbon with Rich Gold. Shade with Burnt Sienna. Dry-brush highlight with Moon Yellow.

Cookie Tin:

1. Base cookie tin with Santa Red. Shade with Black Plum.

2. Base rim, hearts, and lettering with Rich Gold. Highlight with Moon Yellow. Add one-strokes with Dark Pine.

3. Base cookies with Mississippi Mud + Titanium White. Shade with Burnt Sienna. Add frosting around edges with Pearl White.

4. Base snowflakes with Pearl White.

**Santa and Bag Pattern
Enlarge 111%**

Paint the tree shown above as in Trees, Steps 1–4 on pages 29 and 31.

Doll:

1. Base face, hand, and foot with Flesh Tone. Highlight with Titanium White. Shade with Burnt Sienna.

2. Line eyelashes with Asphaltum. Dry-brush cheeks with Santa Red + Flesh Tone. Add mouth with Santa Red.

3. Base hair with Marigold + Santa Red. Line with Burnt Sienna to shade. Line with Marigold to highlight.

4. Base dress with Santa Red + Titanium White. Shade with Black Plum. Highlight with Titanium White.

5. Base sash with Titanium White. Shade with Liberty Blue.

6. Add dots on neckline and bottom of skirt with Titanium White.

Snowman:

1. Base eyes and mouth with Graphite. Shade left sides with Lamp Black. Highlight right sides with Titanium White.

2. Base carrot nose with Marigold + Santa Red. Shade top with Marigold and wash bottom with Santa Red.

3. Base scarf with Dark Pine. Add stripes with Santa Red. Shade with Black Green. Highlight with Bright Green.

4. Line tassels with Santa Red and Dark Pine. Add dots with Santa Red. Shade with Black Plum.

Hat:

1. Base hat with Black Plum. Shade with Lamp Black. Highlight with Santa Red.

2. Base hatband and holly leaves with Dark Pine. Shade with Black Green. Dot berries with Santa Red. Highlight berries with Titanium White. Line leaves with Bright Green. Line veins with Black.

Snow Shovel:

1. Base shovel with Graphite + Titanium White. Shade with Graphite. Dry-brush highlight with Titanium White.

2. Add lettering with Santa Red + Black Plum, making lettering brighter as it moves out of the shade.

3. Base shovel handle with Mississippi Mud. Dry-brush woodgrain with Mississippi Mud + Titanium White, then again with Asphaltum. Shade with Asphaltum.

Snowman Pattern
Enlarge 111%

Paint Palette:

Delta:

Apple Green
Black
Black Green
Cinnamon
Flesh:
    Dark, Medium
Forest Green
Light Ivory
Metallic Gold
Persimmon
Seminole
Tuscan Red

Supplies:

Santa Smoker
    with Tree
Curly Crepe Wool
Sparkle Glaze

Note: When making these descending dots, differently sized "tools" must be used to achieve this effect. I used various paintbrush handles and a stylus.

Note: Substitute curly crepe wool for hair. Add sparkle glaze to beard.

Face:

1. Base face with Medium Flesh. Dry-brush cheeks and nose with Medium Flesh + Tuscan Red.

2. Transfer Eyes Pattern from below onto face.

Eyes Pattern

3. Base lower parts of eyes with Black. Highlight with Apple Green. Add a sparkle with Light Ivory. Softly float around eyes with Dark Flesh. Reverse-float centers of eyelids with Light Ivory.

4. Line eyelashes with Black.

Coat:

1. Base the coat with Tuscan Red. Shade top area and shoulders with Cinnamon. Highlight around middle at wood joint with Persimmon.

2. Transfer scrolls from Coat Scroll Pattern on page 40 onto coat. Do not transfer trees or strokes.

3. Shade inside edges of scrolls with Cinnamon as shown.

4. Transfer trees and strokes from Coat Scroll Pattern onto coat.

5. Line scrolls and stems with Forest Green as shown on page 38. Dry-brush highlight with Seminole, then again with Apple Green.

6. Base trees with Forest Green as shown on page 38. To separate sections, shade with Black Green.

7. Pull tiny lines on tops of shaded areas as shown on page 38. Add tiny one-strokes on edges of sections with Seminole. Add some one-strokes in centers with Apple Green, then a few with Metallic Gold. Add double-loaded reverse teardrops loaded with Persimmon + Light Ivory and

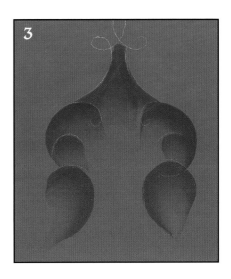

tipped with Cinnamon. Add one-strokes and crosshatching with Metallic Gold.

8. Base holly leaves with Forest Green as shown. Shade with Black Green. Highlight with Apple Green. Line shaded side of each leaf with Metallic Gold. Line veins with Apple Green.

9. Add dots with Persimmon touched with Persimmon + Light Ivory as shown.

Descending Dots:

1. For rows of descending dots down back, mix six values of red—Cinnamon, Cinnamon + Tuscan Red, Tuscan Red, Tuscan Red + Persimmon, Persimmon, Persimmon + Light Ivory. Begin with largest sized dots and make three or four dots with Cinnamon. Using next smaller tool, make three or four more dots with Cinnamon + Tuscan Red. Continue in this manner using a smaller tool each time with a lighter value of color until you have created long chains of dots. Make certain chains of dots are not all the same length. Refer to photo on page 39.

Gloves:

1. Base gloves with Forest Green. Shade next to fur with Black Green. Dry-brush highlight with Seminole, then again with Apple Green.

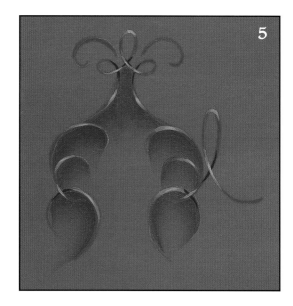

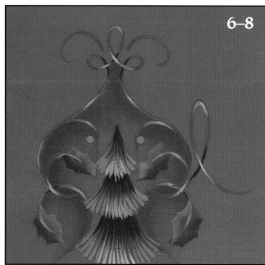

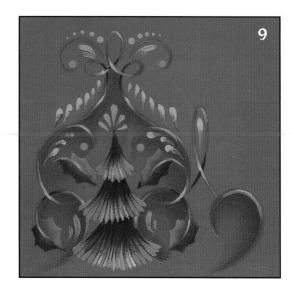

Hat:

1. Shade hat next to fur with Cinnamon. Highlight top with Persimmon, then again with Persimmon + Light Ivory.

2. Transfer Hat Scroll Pattern from page 40 onto hat. Paint design as in Coat, Steps 3 and 5–7 on page 37 and Step 9 at left.

3. Base all fur areas with Light Ivory. Stipple a second coat with Light Ivory. While it is still wet, pick up a small amount of Forest Green and work it into wet paint on outer edges, leaving center area mostly light.

4. For larger fur section on coat, add Forest Green to upper edge and gradually trail it off so bottom edge is straight Light Ivory.

Pants:

1. Base pants with Tuscan Red. Shade under coat with Cinnamon.

2. Base a stripe around lower edge with Forest Green. Dry-brush highlight with Seminole, then again with Apple Green.

3. Add a vertical line down side of each leg with Metallic Gold. Paint scrolls as in Coat, Step 5 on page 37.

Shoes:

1. Base shoes with Cinnamon. Dry-brush highlight toe areas with Tuscan Red, then again with Persimmon, then again with Persimmon + Light Ivory.

2. Very lightly dry-brush with Metallic Gold.

3. Line around soles with Metallic Gold.

Pipe:

1. Base pipe with Forest Green. Shade with Black Green. Dry-brush center front with Apple Green.

2. Line upper edge. Add one-strokes with Metallic Gold.

Bird:

1. Base bird with Tuscan Red. Shade with Cinnamon. Highlight with Persimmon + Light Ivory.

2. Paint beak with Metallic Gold.

3. Add strokes on wings and tail with Persimmon + Light Ivory. Dry-brush highlight head, breast, and back with Metallic Gold.

4. Dot eyes with Black Green.

Tree:

1. Base tree with Forest Green. Dry-brush with Seminole, then again through front area only with Apple Green.

Note: Thin paint so it will soak deep into tree.

2. Add some touches with Metallic Gold.

Base:

1. Base the base with Forest Green. Highlight lower edge with Seminole. Add cross-hatching on top of base with Metallic Gold.

2. Add double-loaded reverse teardrops around routed edge loaded with Persimmon + Light Ivory and tipped with Cinnamon.

Hat Scroll Pattern

Coat Scroll Pattern

SANTA WORKSHOP

Paint Palettes:

Deco Art:
Asphaltum
Black
Black Green
Black Plum
Burnt Orange
Burnt Sienna
Burnt Umber
Buttermilk
Cadmium Red
Evergreen
Flesh Tone
Graphite
Grey Sky
Lamp Black
Light Hauser Green
Metallic Black Pearl
Metallic Silver
Mississippi Mud
Moon Yellow
Navy Blue
Neutral Grey
Raw Sienna
Santa Red
Sapphire
Tangerine
Titanium White

JoSonja:
Pale Gold

Supplies:
Santa's Workshop
    Smoker
Paper Clay

Note: All shading and highlighting floats should be kept "washy" and "layered" for greater color intensity.

Santa:

1. Base shirt with Buttermilk.

2. Wash around suspenders, waistband, cuffs on sleeves, and down button placket on front of shirt with Mississippi Mud. Dry-brush highlight center of button placket with Titanium White. Add connected "S" strokes on sleeves with Neutral Grey.

3. Base lederhosen and socks with Neutral Grey. Stipple ribs on socks with Black Green, then again with Grey Sky.

Note: Hold bristles horizontally when stippling cuff. Hold bristles vertically when stippling below cuff.

4. Shade under cuffs of socks and above shoes with Black Green. Add a stripe on each cuff with Santa Red.

5. To create a soft leather look, dry-brush lederhosen with Grey Sky.

6. Base bands around legs and waist, and suspenders with Evergreen. Shade around front flap and where suspenders overlap pants with Black Green. Highlight with Light Hauser Green. Using "S" strokes, line suspenders with Neutral Grey.

7. To create edelweiss flowers, add double-loaded reverse teardrops on pant legs and suspender crosspiece loaded

with Neutral Grey and tipped with Titanium White. Add some dots in centers with Raw Sienna and some with Moon Yellow. To make leaves, add double-loaded reverse tear-drops loaded with Light Hauser Green and tipped with Evergreen.

8. Base buckles on suspenders with Neutral Grey. Highlight with Metallic Silver. Shade with Metallic Black Pearl.

Santa Face and Beard:

1. Base face with Flesh Tone.

2. Transfer Eyes Pattern from below onto face.

3. Shade around eyes and tops of eyelids with Burnt Sienna as shown. Shade wrinkles on forehead with Burnt Sienna.

4. Highlight wrinkles, bottoms of eyelids, and tops of bags under eyes with Buttermilk as shown.

5. Dry-brush cheeks and top of nose with Santa Red + Flesh Tone.

6. Base eyes with Buttermilk as shown. Add irises with Sapphire. Add pupils with Black "tornadoes." Float highlight left sides of irises with Grey Sky. Add a sparkle to right sides of pupils with Buttermilk.

7. Shade under eyelids across entire eye with Lamp Black as shown. Line eyelashes with Neutral Grey.

8. Knead Neutral Grey acrylic paint into paper clay. Dampen wood with water. Mold hair, eyebrows, beard, and mustache onto Santa's head. Let dry overnight.

Note: Leave top of head bald.

9. Rake in hair with Graphite, then again with Neutral Grey, then again with Buttermilk, then again with Titanium White. Shade with Graphite, making certain to separate hair from beard and under mustache and lip.

10. Highlight eyebrows with Buttermilk, then again with White. Shade with Graphite.

Shoes:

1. Wash shoes with Raw Sienna. Dry-brush highlight on toes with Moon Yellow.

Eyes Pattern

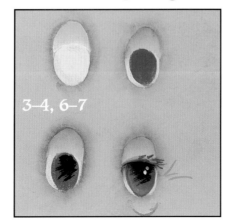

3–4, 6–7

Floor:

1. Base floor with Mississipi Mud + Glazing Medium + Retarder 1:2:$^1/_2$.

2. Using a chalk pencil, lightly mark off $^1/_2$" planks on floor. Float each side of planks with Asphaltum.

3. To create joint lines on planks, randomly float lines to separate planks.

Note: Do not create a pattern as you would with bricks.

Table and Stool:

1. Base tabletop and stool seat with Asphaltum.

2. Wash table legs and stool legs with Evergreen.

Doll:

1. Base face and hands with Flesh Tone. Shade with Burnt Sienna.

2. Dot cheeks and line mouth with Santa Red + Flesh Tone. Add comma-stroke highlight to cheeks with Titanium White.

3. Dot eyes with Sapphire. Shade with Navy Blue. Add a sparkle to eyes with Titanium White. Line eyelashes, eyebrows, and nose with Burnt Sienna.

4. Knead Raw Sienna acrylic paint into a small amount of paper clay. Dampen top of

doll's head with water. Flatten a dime-sized piece of clay and mold hair onto doll's head to create correct hairline. Roll out remaining clay into a long slender strand. Divide strand into three sections and braid. Lay braid across top of doll's hair going from ear to ear. Let dry overnight.

5. Line strands of hair with Moon Yellow. Shade with Raw Sienna. Shade around hairline with Burnt Sienna.

6. Base dress and socks with Buttermilk, painting sleeves to elbows.

7. Base dirndl over dress with Sapphire.

8. Wash apron with Buttermilk. Highlight with White. Shade with Sapphire.

9. Shade blouse and slip with Neutral Grey, sporadically adding small dots around neck, sleeves, along apron, below elbow, and under dirndl with White.

10. Shade dress with Navy Blue. Highlight with Grey Sky.

11. Add buttons down front with Metallic Silver.

12. Line lacing with Buttermilk.

13. Base shoes with Graphite.

Potbelly Stove:

1. Base belly of stove with Graphite.

2. Base chimney pipe and feet with Lamp Black. Drybrush chimney pipe with Graphite.

3. Transfer outline of Door Pattern from below onto stove.

4. Base inside door with Burnt Orange as shown. To make flames, double-load a

Door Pattern

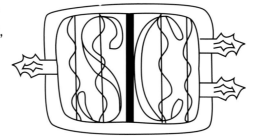

#3 round paintbrush with Tangerine and Santa Red. Shade around inside door with Black Plum.

5. Base door with Graphite + White as shown. Shade with Graphite. Highlight with Metallic Silver.

6. Transfer ironwork detailing from Door Pattern onto door.

7. Line ironwork with Graphite as shown. Highlight with Metallic Black Pearl and Metallic Silver.

8. Base hinges with Metallic Silver as shown. Shade with Black. Shade lip $1/8$" in around top of stove and highlight with Metallic Silver.

9. Shade vents with Black as shown. Highlight with Metallic Silver.

Soldier:

1. Base face and hands with Flesh Tone. Shade with Burnt Sienna.

2. Base hair and gun stock with Burnt Umber. Highlight with Raw Sienna, then again

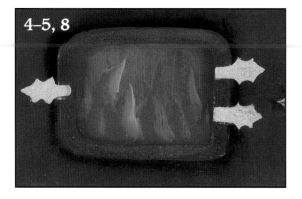

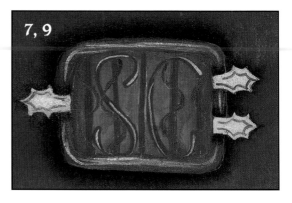

44

with Moon Yellow. Line strokework on gun stock with Raw Sienna. Tip with Pale Gold.

3. Dot cheeks with Santa Red + Flesh Tone.

4. Base hat, chin strap, pants, shoes, belt, and pouch with Black.

5. Stipple hat with Graphite + Neutral Grey. Shade under hat on hair with Asphaltum.

6. Base the coat with Santa Red. Shade with Black Plum.

7. Reverse-float down center of pants with Neutral Grey.

8. Dry-brush belt with Neutral Grey.

9. Line belt buckle, sleeve caps, stripes down pant legs, buttons, and scrollwork on coat with Pale Gold.

Jack-in-the-Box:

1. Base box with Buttermilk.

2. Add ¹/₄"-wide bands around all sides with Evergreen as shown.

3. Paint florals with varying shades of red, blue, and green as shown.

4. Shade inside Buttermilk centers with Raw Sienna as shown. Line strokework with Pale Gold.

5. Base inside top of box with Black Green. Highlight ¹/₈" in from edges with Light Hauser Green.

6. Base face and neck with Flesh Tone. Shade with Burnt Sienna. Dot eyes with Charcoal. Dot cheeks with Santa Red + Flesh Tone. Line mouth with Santa Red.

7. Base spring with Sapphire. Shade with Navy Blue.

8. Knead Burnt Orange acrylic paint into a small amount of paper clay. Dampen top of head with water. Roll out clay into a long slender strand. Lay strand on head in loops. Let dry overnight.

9. Shade hair with Burnt Orange + Burnt Sienna. Highlight with Moon Yellow.

Presents:

1. Base square present with Light Hauser Green.

2. To create diamonds, add thick and thin lines with Buttermilk.

3. Base hearts between diamonds with Santa Red.

4. Base rectangular present with Santa Red. Shade with Black Plum.

5. Line pinstripes with Pale Gold.

2–4

Paintbrush:

1. Base handle with Black Plum and bristles with Raw Sienna.

2. Line bristles with Moon Yellow to separate hairs.

3. Tip bristles with Santa Red.

Paint Jars:

1. Base lids with Grey Sky. Shade with Neutral Grey. Highlight with Titanium White.

2. Base one jar with Evergreen. Highlight with Light Hauser Green.

3. Base one jar with Pale Gold. Shade with Black Plum. Highlight with White.

4. Base one jar with Sapphire. Shade with Navy Blue. Highlight with White.

5. Base remaining jar with Santa Red. Shade with Black Plum. Highlight with White.

Bat:

1. Varnish bat.

Balls and Blocks:

1. Paint balls and blocks as desired.

Drum:

1. Base drum with Buttermilk. Shade with Raw Sienna.

2. Add details with Sapphire. Shade with Navy Blue. Highlight with Grey Sky.

3. Add band around drum with Santa Red.

Note: Leave some of area unfinished.

Train:

1. Base engine and caboose with Santa Red. Shade with Black Plum.

2. Add one-strokes with Pale Gold.

3. Base cattle guard, smokestack, and pistons with Neutral Grey, then again with Metallic Silver. Highlight with Titanium White. Line strokework on cattle guard with Charcoal.

4. Base headlight and bell with Pale Gold. Shade with Burnt Sienna.

5. Base coal car with Neutral Grey. Add strokes with Black.

6. Base passenger car with Evergreen. Shade with Black Green.

7. Base wheels and roofs with Graphite. Add details with Neutral Grey.

8. Base roses with Cadmium Red + Black Plum + Buttermilk. The leaves are double-loaded with Evergreen and Light Hauser Green.

Book:

1. Base book binding with Evergreen. Dry-brush highlight with Light Hauser Green.

2. Base pages with Buttermilk. Shade with Mississippi Mud.

Teddy Bear:

1. Base teddy bear with Raw Sienna. Highlight tummy, paws, and muzzle with Moon Yellow, then again with Buttermilk.

2. Add face detail with Burnt Umber.

Rocking Horse:

Note: Not entirely visible in photo on page 41. Refer to photo on page 52.

1. Base horse with Buttermilk.

2. Base roses with Cadmium Red + Black Plum + Buttermilk as shown. The leaves are double-loaded with Evergreen and Light Hauser Green.

3. Wash saddle with Sapphire as shown. Add crosshatching with Sapphire. Using a 10/0 liner, add double-loaded one-strokes between crosshatching loaded with Cadmium Red and Buttermilk.

4. Base handles with Sapphire.

5. For an antique finish, float around joints with Raw Sienna.

2–3

Finish:

1. Using a hot-glue gun, glue ribbons on teddy bear and jack-in-the-box. Glue beads to table. Glue assorted "goodies" inside goodie bag.

QUILTED SNOWMEN

Paint Palette:

Deco Art:
Black Forest Green
Blue Mist
Buttermilk
Cadmium Red
Cranberry Wine
Dark Pine
Graphite
Lamp Black
Marigold
Midnight Blue
Mistletoe
Moon Yellow
Raw Sienna
Santa Red
Titanium White
Wedgewood Blue

Supplies:

Wooden Snowman
    Nutcracker
Wooden Snowman
    Smoker
Wooden Buttons (3)
Snowflake Button
Fantasy Snow (Delta)

*Note: All shading
and highlighting floats
should be kept "washy"
and "layered" for
greater color intensity.*

Snowmen:

1. Base snowmen with Blue Mist.

2. Sponge snowmen with Titanium White + Glazing Medium 1:2.

Note: Repeat two to three more times until desired "whiteness" is achieved.

Eyes:

1. Base eyes with Graphite.

2. Shade under eyes with Blue Mist.

3. Shade inside left sides of eyes with Lamp Black.

4. Highlight inside right edges of eyes with Blue Mist.

5. Add a sparkle to eyes with Titanium White.

Noses:

1. Base noses with Marigold, then wash with Cadmium Red.

2. Dry-brush with Moon Yellow.

Mouths:

1. Base nutcracker's mouth with Raw Sienna. Shade with Raw Sienna + Graphite.

2. Shade under mouth with Blue Mist. Highlight with Raw Sienna + Buttermilk, then again with Buttermilk.

Hat and Vest:

1. Transfer Vest Pattern from below onto smoker snowman. Divide vest and hat into sections.

2. Alternately base patches on vest and hat with Santa Red, Buttermilk, Dark Pine, and Wedgewood Blue.

Vest Pattern

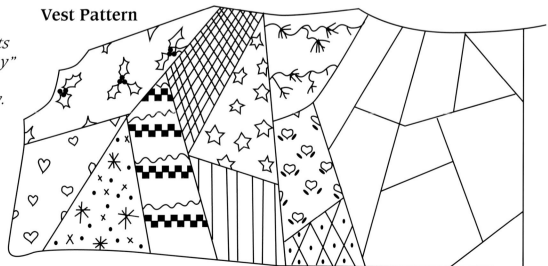

3. Add details to patches as desired.

4. Shade around each Santa Red patch with Cranberry Wine, each Buttermilk patch with Graphite, each Dark Pine patch with Black Forest Green, and each Wedgewood Blue patch with Midnight Blue.

5. Base hatband with Wedgewood Blue. Highlight with Blue Mist. Shade with Midnight Blue.

6. Line around vest with Santa Red. Highlight center with Cadmium Red. Shade behind vest with Blue Mist.

Buttons:

1. Base red buttons with Santa Red. Shade centers with Cranberry Wine. Dry-brush highlight with Cadmium Red + Moon Yellow.

2. Base green buttons with Dark Pine. Shade centers with Black Forest Green. Dry-brush highlight with Mistletoe + Moon Yellow.

3. Base blue buttons with Wedgewood Blue. Shade centers with Midnight Blue. Dry-brush highlight with Blue Mist.

Birdhouse:

1. Base birdhouse with Santa Red. To make woodgrain, streak with Cranberry Wine, then again with Cadmium Red.

2. Base chimney and perch with Graphite. Shade with Lamp Black. Base top of chimney with Santa Red. Shade with Cranberry Wine.

3. Base roof and platform with Black Forest Green. Paint checkerboard on platform with Buttermilk.

4. Dot berries around front edge of roof with Santa Red. Add leaves with Mistletoe.

5. Using a 1/4" filbert rake, add shingles with Mistletoe.

6. Add snow as desired.

51

Paint Palettes:

Deco Art:
Asphaltum
Black Green
Black Plum
Bright Green
Burnt Sienna
Buttermilk
Evergreen
Flesh Tone
Grey Sky
Lamp Black
Marigold
Midnight Blue
Mississippi Mud
Mistletoe
Moon Yellow
Santa Red
Silver Sage Green
Titanium White
Wedgewood Blue

Delta:
Hippo Grey

JoSonja:
Pale Gold

Supplies:

Wooden Toy Vendor
   Nutcracker

*Note: All shading
and highlighting floats
should be kept "washy"
and "layered" for
greater color intensity.*

Base:

1. To create cobblestones, slip-slap base with small amounts of Hippo Grey, Grey Sky, Mississippi Mud, and Black Plum.

Note: Work back and forth between colors.

2. Line between stones with Black Green, making certain stones are not identical.

3. Dry-brush highlight on some stones with Grey Sky.

4. Shade around stones with Asphaltum, Black Green, and Black Plum, making certain stones are not identical.

5. Splatter with Titanium White thinned with Flow Medium.

6. Transfer Poinsettia Scroll Pattern from page 57 onto front of base.

7. Paint poinsettia as in Hatband, Steps 2–4 on page 54. Paint holly leaves, berries, scrolls, stems, and veins as in Tray, Steps 5–7 on page 56.

Hat:

1. Base hat with Black Green.

2. Sponge with Hippo Grey + Glazing Medium (1:2) as shown, then again with Hippo Grey, Silver Sage Green + Glazing Medium (1:1:2), then again with Silver Sage Green + Glazing Medium (1:2). Glaze with Evergreen.

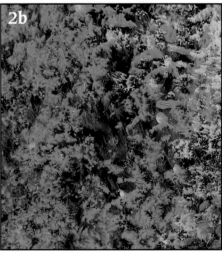

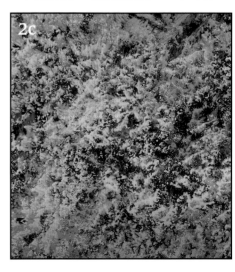

Hatband:

1. Base hatband with Black Green. Shade above and below hatband on hat with Black Green.

2. Layer leaves with Evergreen, then again with Mistletoe, then again with Bright Green as shown. Line leaves and veins with Silver Sage Green.

3. Layer poinsettias with Black Plum, then again with Santa Red, then again with Santa Red + Marigold as shown. Line poinsettias with Santa Red + Titanium White.

4. Add dots in centers with Marigold as shown. Highlight with Titanium White.

Note: Leaves and petals are loose strokes, one on top of the other.

Mittens:

1. Base mittens with Black Plum. Stipple highlights with Santa Red, then again with Santa Red + Marigold.

Double-breasted Coat:

1. Base the coat with Hippo Grey.

2. To create the double-breast, highlight from bottom right side of mouth opening to bottom of coat with Silver Sage Green. Shade next to highlight with Black Green.

3. Dot six buttons with Santa Red. Shade with Black Plum. Shade behind bottom edges of buttons with Black Green.

Pants, Lapel, and Elbow Pads:

1. Base pants, lapel, and elbow pads with Silver Sage Green. Base pant cuffs with Hippo Grey. Dry-brush highlight in centers of cuffs with Silver Sage Green.

2. To create herringbone, place ¼"-wide tape vertically every ¼" across pants. Rake diagonally with Evergreen, then again with Black Green, then again with Black Plum as shown. Let dry, then remove tape. Tape over raked area. Repeat, raking in opposite direction. Let dry, then remove tape. Shade with Black Green.

3. Line and add stitching around elbow patches with Black Plum.

Shoes:

1. Base shoes with Asphaltum. Shade around bottoms of shoes with Lamp Black. Dry-brush highlight tops of shoes with Asphaltum + Titanium White.

Face:

1. Base face with Flesh Tone. Shade under hat, above eyes as shown, and below eyebrows with Burnt Sienna.

2. Dry-brush cheeks and top of nose with Santa Red + Flesh Tone. Highlight above cheeks with Buttermilk.

3. Transfer Eyes Pattern from below onto face.

4. Base eyes with Buttermilk as shown. Add irises with Grey Sky. Shade around irises with Wedgewood Blue. Add pupils with Lamp Black. Highlight with Titanium White. Add a sparkle to eyes with Titanium White. Shade across eyes with Lamp Black.

Eyes Pattern

5. Line eyelashes and eyebrows with Asphaltum as shown. Highlight lines on eyebrows with Buttermilk.

6. Base lips with Santa Red. Base teeth with Buttermilk. Shade with Hippo Grey. Highlight with Titanium White. Line teeth with Hippo Grey. Add a sparkle on lips with Titanium White.

1, 4–5

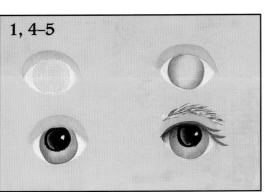

55

Tray:

1. Wash tray with Asphaltum. Mark ¼" from bottom of tray and base area with Black Green.

2. Paint checkerboard with Mistletoe.

3. Transfer Heart Scroll Pattern from below onto front of tray.

4. Base heart with Santa Red. Shade with Black Plum.

5. Base holly leaves with Evergreen. Line with Mistletoe + Silver Sage Green.

6. Dot some berries with Black Plum and some with Santa Red.

7. Line scrolls, stems, and veins with Evergreen.

Heart Scroll Pattern

Sign:

1. Wash sign with Asphaltum. Add broken line around sign with Black Green.

2. Transfer Sign Pattern from below onto sign.

3. Base "Toys" with Santa Red. Line right side and bottom with Black Plum. Highlight left side with Santa Red + Marigold.

4. Base "for sale" with Mistletoe. Line with Evergreen.

5. Paint poinsettia as in Hatband, Steps 2–4 on page 54. Paint holly leaves, berries, stems, and veins as in Tray, Steps 5–7 above.

Rocking Horse:

1. Base horse with Grey Sky. Shade with Lamp Black + Grey Sky.

2. Base roses with Cadmium Red + Black Plum + Buttermilk. The leaves are double-loaded with Evergreen and Mistletoe.

3. Shade saddle with Wedgewood Blue. Add crosshatching with Wedgewood Blue. Using a 10/0 liner, add double-loaded one-strokes between crosshatching loaded with Cadmium Red and Buttermilk.

4. Base handles with Pale Gold.

5. Line scrolls on rockers with Pale Gold.

Sign Pattern

Teddy Bear:

1. Base teddy bear with Burnt Sienna. Stipple with Marigold + Burnt Sienna, then again with Marigold, then again with Moon Yellow. Highlight with Buttermilk.

2. Stipple insides of ears with Santa Red + Buttermilk.

3. Add face detail with Lamp Black.

Soldier:

1. Base face and hands with Flesh Tone. Shade with Burnt Sienna.

2. Base hair with Burnt Umber. Highlight with Raw Sienna.

3. Dot eyes with Lamp Black. Highlight with Titanium White. Dry-brush cheeks with Santa Red + Flesh Tone. Line nose with Burnt Sienna. Line mouth with Santa Red.

4. Base hat with Lamp Black. Stipple with Hippo Grey. Base chin strap with Lamp Black.

5. Base the coat with Santa Red. Shade with Black Plum. Highlight with Santa Red + Marigold.

6. Base pants with Hippo Grey. Reverse-float down center of pants with Lamp Black.

7. Line belt buckle, sleeve caps, buttons, and scrollwork on hat and coat with Pale Gold.

Toy Nutcracker:

1. Base hat with Midnight Blue. Stipple with Wedgewood, then again with Grey Sky.

2. Base face and hands with Flesh Tone. Shade with Burnt Sienna.

3. Base hair with Burnt Sienna. Highlight with Moon Yellow.

4. Base eyes with Lamp Black. Dry-brush cheeks with Santa Red + Flesh Tone. Line mouth with Santa Red.

Poinsettia Scroll Pattern

5. Base the coat with Wedgewood Blue. Shade with Midnight Blue. Highlight with Grey Sky.

6. Base cuffs, pants, and shirt with Grey Sky. Shade with Wedgewood Blue.

7. Base belt and shoes with Lamp Black. Add details with Pale Gold.

Train:

1. Base bottoms of engine, coal car, passenger car, and caboose with Lamp Black.

2. Base cattle guard and smokestack on engine, entire coal car, and pigeon roost on caboose with Grey Sky. Shade with Wedgewood Blue + Lamp Black.

3. Add vertical one-strokes on cattle guard with Wedgewood Blue + Lamp Black. Highlight between vertical one-strokes with Titanium White.

4. Base engine cabin and passenger cabin with Mistletoe. Highlight with Bright Green. Shade with Evergreen. Add details with Pale Gold.

5. Base engine and caboose with Santa Red. Highlight with Santa Red + Marigold. Shade with Black Plum. Add details with Pale Gold.

6. Base headlight, bell, and top light on engine with Moon Yellow. Shade with Burnt Sienna. Highlight with Pale Gold.

7. Base wheels and roofs with Hippo Grey. Dot wheels with Santa Red, adding a smaller dot with Black Plum.

8. Add crosshatching on roofs and shingles with Silver Sage Green. Shade with Black Green.

Paint Palettes:

Deco Art:
Emperor's Gold

Delta:
Black
Black Green
Blue Storm
Burnt Umber
Cadet Blue
Dark Forest
Flesh: Dark, Medium
Forest Green
Green Sea
Light Ivory
Maple Sugar
Old Parchment
Pearl Luster
Raw Sienna
Tide Pool Blue
Tuscan Red
White

JoSonja:
Pale Gold

Supplies:

14" Single-bead Scoop
  Wooden Plate

©2001 Kristen Birkeland, CDA

Plate:

1. Base plate with Tide Pool Blue.

2. Apply Retarder over plate. Beginning at center of plate, slip-slap with a large flat paintbrush double-loaded with Cadet Blue and Tide Pool Blue.

Note: Brush in short blending strokes in all directions. If necessary, use more Retarder. The background should look softly mottled, not streaky. Use a mop to soften and blend.

3. Double-load paintbrush with Tide Pool Blue and Tide Pool Blue + Light Ivory and continue toward outer edges.

Note: Paint should gradually get lighter toward edges.

4. Base outer rim with Blue Storm. Dry-brush with Pearl Luster.

5. Transfer Angel Pattern from page 63 onto plate.

Note: Do not transfer holly leaves at this time.

Dress:

1. Base dress with two or three coats of White.

2. Apply Retarder over dress. Beginning at bottom of dress, float stripes with a Tuscan Red wash, letting paint fade out at top of stripes. Use a mop to soften and blend. Let dry.

3. Shade stripes where they go under drape and behind banner with the Tuscan Red wash. Line sprigs with Emperor's Gold.

4. Shade inside sleeves and behind drape with a soft Tide Pool Blue wash. Darken inside sleeves and around dove with a small amount of Cadet Blue.

5. Lightly wash over dress with Pearl Luster + White + a small amount of Tide Pool Blue.

6. Highlight edges of sleeves and bodice with Pearl Luster.

Drape:

1. Base drape with Tide Pool Blue.

2. Beginning at shoulder area, gradually darken with Cadet Blue. The shadows should extend down to about the waist before blending into Tide Pool Blue base. Repeat as necessary. Lighten lower edge, gradually working upward, with Tide Pool Blue + Light Ivory.

3. Shade lightest areas with Cadet Blue. Shade darkest areas with Blue Storm.

4. Highlight with Tide Pool Blue, then again with Tide Pool Blue + Light Ivory.

5. Base stars with Pearl Luster.

Note: Stars should be very small at top and get larger toward center of drape.

Banner:

1. Base banner with Blue Storm. Shade with Blue Storm + Black. Dry-brush highlight with Tide Pool Blue, then again with Tide Pool Blue + Light Ivory.

2. Line edges with Emperor's Gold.

3. Add lettering with Tide Pool Blue. Highlight with Pearl Luster.

Face and Hands:

1. Base entire head, neck, and hands with Medium Flesh. Shade with Dark Flesh.

2. Dry-brush cheeks with Medium Flesh + Tuscan Red.

3. Base eyes with Light Ivory. Add irises with Cadet Blue. Highlight with Tide Pool Blue. Add pupils with tiny lines of Black. Add a sparkle to eyes with Light Ivory.

4. Line mouth with Dark Flesh + Tuscan Red.

Hair:

1. Line hair with Raw Sienna. Add a few lines of Burnt Umber. Shade behind curls and next to face and neck with Burnt Umber. Highlight with Maple Sugar, then again with Old Parchment. Add a few lines of Emperor's Gold.

2. Base holly leaves with Forest Green. Line with Green Sea. Dot some berries with Tuscan Red and some with Pearl Luster.

Halo:

1. Apply Retarder over area around head. Using a large flat paintbrush, highlight next to hair with Emperor's Gold.

2. Using a mop or dry paintbrush, pull the wet paint from head outward.

3. Add tiny dots along outer edge of halo with Pale Gold.

Dove:

1. Base dove with White. Shade with Tide Pool Blue. Highlight with Pearl Luster.

2. Line eye with Black, beak with Emperor's Gold, and olive branch with Forest Green.

Holly Garland Ribbon:

1. Using Holly Leaf Patterns on page 63, randomly stencil holly leaves along main stem lines with Dark Forest, Forest Green + Green Sea, and Green Sea.

2. Line some leaves with Black Green.

3. Line stem with Dark Forest.

4. Dot some berries with Tuscan Red and some with Pearl Luster.

5. Add ribbon, woven in and out of holly garland, with the Tuscan Red wash, a Pearl Luster wash, and a Cadet Blue wash.

Each year for the past 11 years, I have designed a plate to be used in a traditional cookie exchange. Last year, I decided that ten years was a good time to stop. But after the events of September 11, 2001, I decided to design one final plate in honor of Americans and all those who fight for peace.

—Kristen

Angel Pattern
Enlarge 117%

Holly Leaf
Patterns
Enlarge 117%

Peace On Earth Good Will To Men

PINECONE TISSUE BOX

Paint Palette:

Delta:
Apple Green
Black Green
Burnt Umber
Cinnamon
Dark Brown
Dark Burnt Umber
Flesh Tan
Forest Green
Fruit Punch
Leaf Green
Light Ivory
Maple Sugar
Moroccan Red
Old Parchment
Pine Green
Raw Sienna
Spice Tan
White

Supplies:
Wooden Tissue Box
  with Lid

Tissue Box:

1. Base tissue box and lid with two or three coats of Light Ivory.

2. Tape off all Light Ivory vertical stripes around tissue box and base untaped areas with Pine Green as shown in Diagram A below. Let dry, then remove tape.

3. Add one thin stripe around sides of lid with Pine Green. Add one thin stripe around opening in box lid with Moroccan Red.

Ribbon:

1. Transfer Pinecone Swag Pattern from page 66 onto tissue box.

2. Base ribbon with Moroccan Red as shown on page 66. Highlight with Fruit Punch.

3. Lighten highlights with Fruit Punch + a small amount of Light Ivory as shown on page 66. Shade with Cinnamon. Darken shading with Cinnamon + Pine Green.

Pinecones:

1. Base bottom pinecone with Dark Brown as shown on page 66. Shade under small petals and around outer edges with Burnt Umber.

2. Side-load a small flat paintbrush with Maple Sugar and highlight petals by standing paintbrush on its chisel edge as shown on page 66. Set it down on edges of petals and slightly pull paintbrush back. Apply several of these strokes to each petal.

3. To further highlight, repeat on center petals with Old Parchment as shown on page 66.

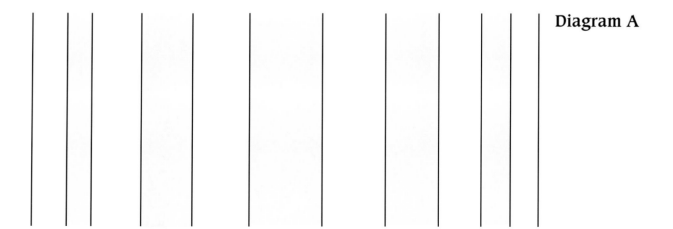

Diagram A

4. Base top pinecone with Raw Sienna as shown. Stipple highlight in center with Spice Tan, then again with Spice Tan + Light Ivory.

5. Divide sections with "wiggly" lines of Dark Brown as shown. Shade above lines in both directions and around outer edges with Burnt Umber.

6. Highlight in centers of middle petals with a small amount of Flesh Tan as shown.

7. Darken between pinecones and next to ribbon with Dark Burnt Umber as shown.

Pine Sprigs:

1. Line main stems for pine sprigs around bow with Pine Green as shown.

2. Pulling needles from each stem line outward, add a layer of needles to each stem with

Pinecone Swag Pattern

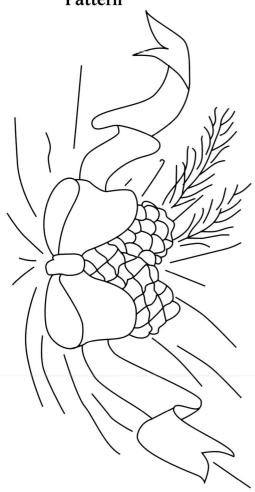

2–3;
1–7;
1–8

Pine Green as shown. Let a few "tips" cross over to top of lid. Add a second layer of needles with Forest Green.

3.   Shade next to bow with Pine Green as shown. To separate some of the sprigs, float irregular lines across them with Black Green, thus creating two separate branches.

4.   If too much Light Ivory background is showing through, lightly wash over sprigs with Pine Green as shown.

5.   Pulling in opposite direction—from tip of needle back toward main stem—add a layer of needles with Leaf Green as shown. Make certain to cover hard Black Green float with tips of strokes.

Note: This layer should not go all the way back to base of branch. The strokes should be short and stay on tips.

6.   Add a few more needles on tips with Apple Green as shown.

Note: If you have holes, add another branch until you have balance.

7.   Darken some of the tight corners around bow with Black Green as shown.

8.   Dot berries with Light Ivory as shown. Shade with Leaf Green. Highlight with White.

Paint Palettes:

Deco Art:
Napa Red
Olive Green
Tomato Red

Delta:
Black Green
Burnt Sienna
Dark Jungle
Leaf Green
Maple Sugar
Old Parchment
Raw Sienna
Seminole
Spice Tan
White

JoSonja:
Cadmium Scarlet

Supplies:

Wooden Memory Book

Scrapbook:

1. Base scrapbook with Dark Jungle. Lightly sponge with Dark Jungle + Black Green, then again with Dark Jungle + Seminole. Float around outer edges with Black Green—do not float edges where hinges go.

2. Base cut edges of scrapbook with Tomato Red.

Band:

1. Transfer Scrapbook Pattern from page 71 onto scrapbook.

2. Base octagonal band with Spice Tan. Reverse-float shade corners with Raw Sienna, then again with Burnt Sienna. Reverse-float highlight center of each section with Maple Sugar, then again with Old Parchment.

3. Shade around both edges of band with Black Green.

Bow:

1. Base bow with Tomato Red + White, then again with Tomato Red. Dry-brush highlight with Cadmium Scarlet. Shade with Napa Red. Darken shading with Napa Red + Dark Jungle.

Lettering:

1. Base lettering with Tomato Red + White, then again with Tomato Red. Dry-brush highlight with Cadmium Scarlet. Shade behind some lettering with Black Green.

2. Base holly leaves and stems with Seminole. Highlight with Leaf Green, then again with Olive Green.

3. Line veins with Dark Jungle. Shade behind some leaves with Black Green.

4. Dot some berries with Cadmium Scarlet and some with White.

Holly Corners:

1. Line corners with Tomato Red.

2. Paint holly leaves on corner lines as in Lettering, Steps 2–4 above.

3. Dry-brush between leaves with Cadmium Scarlet.

Bells:

1. Base bells with Maple Sugar.

2. Wash over bells with Raw Sienna.

3. Dry-brush highlight with Old Parchment, then again with Old Parchment + White, then again with White.

4. Shade with Raw Sienna, then again with Burnt Sienna, then again with a small amount of Napa Red. Shade behind bells with Black Green. Dots holes in bells with Napa Red.

5. Line cord with Seminole.

6. Add tiny "S" strokes over Seminole with Leaf Green. Highlight with Olive Green, then again with Olive Green + White.

Scrapbook Pattern
 Enlarge 111%

Paint Palettes:

Delta:
Apple Green
Black
Black Green
Burnt Umber
Cadet Blue
Cinnamon
Dark Forest Green
Empire Gold
Flesh:
 Dark, Medium
Forest Green
Leaf Green
Metallic Bronze
Seminole
Spice Brown
Spice Tan
Tomato Spice
White

JoSonja:
Cadmium Scarlet

Supplies:

Wooden Music Box

©2002 Kristen Birkeland, CDA

Santa:

1. Base face with Medium Flesh.

2. Dry-brush cheeks and nose with Medium Flesh + Tomato Spice.

3. Dot eyes with Black.

4. Base hat, coat, and pants with Tomato Spice. Shade next to fur areas with Cinnamon.

5. Dry-brush highlight tops of hat, shoulders, and back with Cadmium Scarlet.

6. Line trees in border with Seminole as shown. Highlight with Apple Green.

7. Line snowflakes and add dots with White as shown.

8. Add reverse teardrops with Cadmium Scarlet as shown.

9. Base all fur areas with Cadet Blue as shown. Stipple with White.

10. Base mittens with Forest Green. Shade with Black Green. Paint design as in Step 6 above.

11. Base boots with Black. Dry-brush highlight with Cadet Blue + White.

73

Base:

1. Wash floor area with Spice Brown. Float around outer edge with Burnt Umber. Base outer area with Tomato Spice.

2. Using a crumpled piece of plastic wrap, pounce over outer area with Cadmium Scarlet + Retarder as shown.

3. Add double-loaded reverse teardrops loaded with Leaf Green and tipped with Dark Forest Green as shown.

4. Line snowflakes and add dots with White as shown.

5. Paint bands and all knobs with Metallic Bronze as shown.

Trees:

1. Base trees with Forest Green.

2. Shade under each bough section with Black Green.

3. Stipple lower edge of each bough with Seminole, then again with Leaf Green, then again with a small amount of Apple Green.

4. Dot ornaments on largest tree with Metallic Bronze. Dot ornaments on medium-sized tree as shown in photo on page 73 with Cadmium Scarlet.

Soldier:

1. Base hat with Black. Dry-brush highlight with Cadet Blue. Add one-strokes and dot with Metallic Bronze.

2. Base face with Medium Flesh.

3. Dry-brush cheeks with Medium Flesh + Tomato Spice.

4. Base hair with Black. Highlight with Cadet Blue. Line eyes and moustache with Black.

5. Base the coat with Tomato Spice.

6. Base pants, boots, and belt with Black. Highlight boots with White.

7. Add buttons, belt buckle, and strokes on sleeves with Metallic Bronze.

8. Base gloves with White.

Elves:

1. Base heads and arms with Medium Flesh. Shade with Dark Flesh.

2. Dry-brush cheeks with Medium Flesh + Tomato Spice.

3. Line noses and mouths with Dark Flesh + Tomato Spice.

4. Dot eyes with Black. Highlight with White. Line eyebrows with Black.

5. Base clothes with varying shades of red and green. Add accents with Metallic Bronze.

6. Base hammer head with Black + White. Shade with Black + White. Highlight with White. Wash handle with Spice Brown.

Train:

1. Base train as desired.

2. Add details with contrasting colors.

Teddy Bear:

1. Base teddy bear with Spice Tan.

2. Lightly stipple with Spice Tan + White.

3. Shade around body, muzzle, neck, and insides of ears with Spice Brown.

4. Stipple highlights on tips of ears, muzzle, hands, and feet with Spice Tan + White (1:2).

5. Line eyes, nose, and mouth with Black.

6. Line a bow around neck with Cadmium Scarlet.

Finish:

1. Using a hot-glue gun, glue hair and beard on Santa. Glue hair and hats on elves.

2. Assemble as shown in photos on pages 72–74.

MATCH HOLDER

Paint Palettes:

Delta:

Apple Green
Black
Black Green
Burnt Umber
Cadet Blue
Cinnamon
Dark Forest Green
Empire Gold
Leaf Green
Light Ivory
Metallic Bronze
Moroccan Red
Pale Gold
Seminole
Spice Brown
Spice Tan

JoSonja:

Cadmium Scarlet

Supplies:

Wooden Match Holder
Old Masters®
    Finishing Stain,
    Early American

*Note: Stain wood
prior to painting.*

Match Holder:

1. Shade edges and corners, except front corner where feather tree will be, with Burnt Umber.

2. Base cut edges with Dark Forest Green.

3. Line top and sides with Metallic Bronze.

Feather Tree:

1. Transfer Feather Tree Pattern from page 79 onto corner of match holder.

2. Dry-brush area where star and candle flames will be with Metallic Bronze.

3. Base star with Empire Gold. Shade center with Metallic Bronze. Highlight tips with Pale Gold + a small amount of Metallic Bronze.

4. Base trunk and branches with Spice Brown. Line ribbon spiraled around trunk with Moroccan Red.

5. Add first layer of needles with Dark Forest Green, pulling strokes from branches outward as shown. Add second layer of needles with Seminole.

6. Pull a few needles from trunk outward with Black Green as shown. Highlight tips of needles with short strokes of Leaf Green pulled in the opposite direction— from tips inward.

7. Add highlight strokes on "tips" and "tops" of each branch with Apple Green as shown.

Hearts and Candles:

1. Base hearts with Moroccan Red as shown. Highlight with Cadmium Scarlet. Shade with Cinnamon.

2. Base candles with Light Ivory as shown. Wash with a Pale Gold wash.

3. Base flames with Empire Gold as shown. Shade at flames' bases with Moroccan Red. Highlight tips with Pale Gold.

4. Line wicks with Black as shown.

Candy Cane:

1. Base candy cane with Light Ivory.

2. Add stripes alternately with Moroccan Red and Leaf Green. Lightly shade edges with Cadet Blue. Highlight with Light Ivory.

Gingerbread Boy:

1. Base gingerbread boy with Spice Tan. Dry-brush highlight through center with Spice Tan + Light Ivory. Shade edges with Spice Brown.

2. Dot eyes and buttons with Burnt Umber.

3. Line icing line with Light Ivory.

4. Line mouth and bow with Moroccan Red. Highlight bow with Cadmium Scarlet.

Heart-shaped Basket:

1. Base and add details to woven heart-shaped basket with combinations of red, green, and white.

Note: It may be necessary to touch up some of the needles so items appear to be "hanging" over branches.

Birdhouse:

1. Base birdhouse with Spice Brown. Shade under roof, along bottom, and add hole with Burnt Umber.

2. Base roof with Moroccan Red. Highlight with Cadmium Scarlet.

3. Stipple wreath around hole with Dark Forest Green, then again with Leaf Green, then again with a small amount of Apple Green. Dot berries and add bow with Moroccan Red. Highlight bow with Cadmium Scarlet.

Tree Planter:

1. Base planter with Moroccan Red. Highlight center with Cadmium Scarlet. Shade sides with Cinnamon.

2. Transfer holly design from Feather Tree Pattern onto front of planter.

3. Base holly leaves with Dark Forest Green. Highlight with Leaf Green, then again with Apple Green.

4. Dot berries with Cadmium Scarlet.

5. Line leaves and veins with Metallic Bronze.

6. Add one-strokes with Metallic Bronze.

Presents:

1. Base presents and ribbons randomly with Moroccan Red and varying shades of green.

2. Highlight ribbons with Metallic Bronze.

Feather Tree Pattern

80

SLEIGH

Paint Palettes:

Deco Art:
Black Green
Black Plum
Bright Green
Cranberry Wine
Evergreen
Grey Sky
Mistletoe
Moon Yellow
Santa Red
Titanium White

Delta:
Adriatic Blue
Midnight Blue

JoSonja:
Pale Gold
Rich Gold

Supplies:

Wooden Sleigh

Note: All shading and highlighting floats should be kept "washy" and "layered" for greater color intensity.

Top and Bottom of Sleigh including Runners:

1. Base top and bottom of sleigh and both runners with Adriatic Blue.

2. Base edge of sleigh top and spindle between runners with Midnight Blue.

3. Add lettering around edge of sleigh top with Rich Gold. Add snowflakes with Titanium White.

4. Transfer Bell and Ribbon Pattern from page 83 onto top of sleigh. Transfer Pine Tree Landscape Pattern from page 83 onto runners.

Ribbons:

1. Base ribbons with Cranberry Wine. Dry-brush highlight with Santa Red, then again with Santa Red + Moon Yellow, then again with Santa Red + Moon Yellow (1:2).

2. Glaze over entire ribbon with Santa Red + Glazing Medium. Shade with Black Plum.

3. Using the hit/skip method, line with Black Plum.

Pine Sprigs:

1. Base area where sprigs will be with Retarder. Base with Evergreen. Use a mop to soften and blend.

2. Line main stems for pine sprigs around bow with Black Green.

3. Pulling needles from each stem line outward, add a layer of needles to each stem with Evergreen. Add a second layer of needles with Mistletoe.

4. To separate some of the sprigs, float irregular lines across them with Black Green, thus creating two separate branches.

5. Pulling in opposite direction—from tip of needle back toward main stem—add a layer of needles with Bright Green. Make certain to cover hard Black Green floats with tips of strokes. This layer should not go all the way back to stem or center of sprig.

6. Add a few more needles on tips with Bright Green + Moon Yellow.

7. Shade behind ribbon and bells with Black Green.

Bells:

1. Base bottom bell with Black Plum and remaining bells with Cranberry Wine.

2. Base over all three bells with Rich Gold. Line centers with Pale Gold.

3. Shade bottom bell with Black Plum. Shade remaining bells with Cranberry Wine. Highlight with Pale Gold. Add reflected light on each bell with Titanium White + Adriatic Blue.

4. Add holes on bells with Black Plum. Highlight left sides of holes with Cranberry Wine.

5. Add sprigs over ribbons and bells as in Pine Sprigs, Steps 1–6 on page 81.

Seat Back:

1. Base bottom piece of seat back with Evergreen. Using a #2 flat paintbrush, base checkerboard onto top with Adriatic Blue. Float holly leaves with Bright Green. Line leaves and veins with Bright Green. Dot berries with Santa Red. Shade with Black Plum.

2. Base top piece of seat back with Santa Red, then again with two coats of Cranberry Wine. Alternately line plaid pattern with Santa Red, Adriatic Blue, Mistletoe, and Rich Gold. Base hearts with Santa Red. Highlight with Santa Red + Moon Yellow. To make leaves, add double-loaded reverse teardrops loaded with Bright Green and tipped with Evergreen.

3. Alternately base spindles with Santa Red, Bright Green, and Adriatic Blue.

Pine Tree Landscape:

1. Float hills with Grey Sky. Dry-brush tops of hills and tops and bottoms of runners with Titanium White. Darken behind some hills with Midnight Blue.

2. Line trunks and main branches on trees with Black Green, then again with Evergreen. Highlight center trees by lining tips of branches with Mistletoe, then again with Grey Sky. Highlight foreground trees by lining tips of branches with Bright Green, then again with Titanium White.

3. Splatter runners and top of sleigh with Titanium White.

Bell and Ribbon Pattern

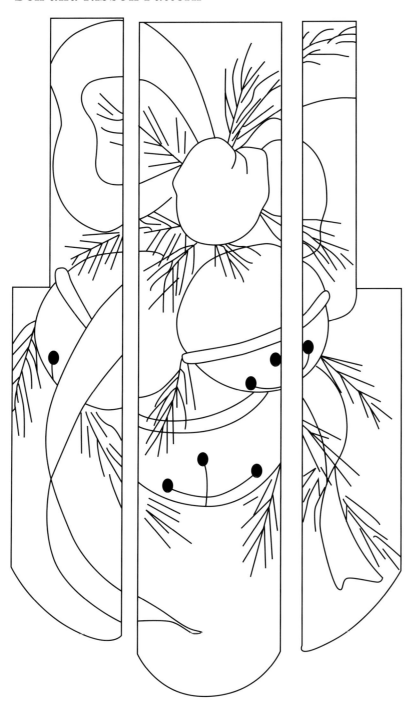

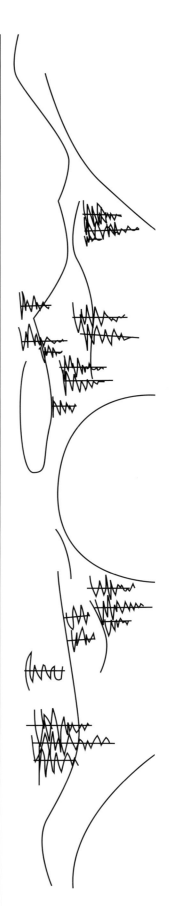

Pine Tree Landscape Pattern

84

Paint Palettes:

Deco Art:
Black Plum
Burnt Sienna
Buttermilk
Charcoal Grey
Cranberry Wine
Flesh Tone
Forest Green
Lamp Black
Raw Sienna
Santa Red
Taffy Cream
Titanium White

Delta:
Maple Sugar

JoSonja:
Pale Gold
Rich Gold

Supplies:

Wooden Nutcrackers
Wig: #812 S, 19 cm,
   colour #20
Ribbon

*Note: All shading
and highlighting floats
should be kept "washy"
and "layered" for
greater color intensity.*

Princess Clara—

Dress:

1. Mark bodice sash and ruffle lines with a pencil.

2. Wash over dress and sleeves with Raw Sienna as shown.

3. Rake over dress with Maple Sugar + Glazing Medium, then again with Taffy Cream + Glazing Medium, then again with Buttermilk + Glazing Medium as shown.

4. Add highlights with Titanium White + Glazing Medium as shown.

Note: Apply highlights more heavily near top and at ruffle line. Apply fewer highlights in areas you want to be in shadows of gathers.

5. Wash over entire dress with Pale Gold + Glazing Medium as shown. Shade along ruffle with Raw Sienna, then again with Rich Gold, ruffling paintbrush as you float. Shade along both sides of sash with Raw Sienna, then again with Rich Gold.

6. Highlight top of ruffle on skirt with Titanium White. Reverse-float highlight with Rich Gold $1/4"$ below top of ruffle, ruffling paintbrush as you float.

7. Base insides of pleats on sleeves with Rich Gold.

8. Line holly leaves above and below each pleat and line veins with Rich Gold.

9. Dot berries with Cranberry Wine. Highlight a few with Santa Red + Titanium White.

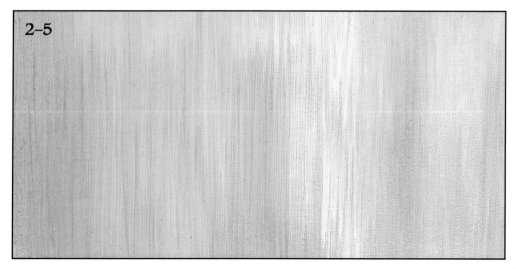

2–5

Face:

1. Base face, neck, hands, and wrists with Flesh Tone. Shade with Burnt Sienna.

2. Transfer Princess' Face Pattern from below onto face.

3. Dampen cheeks with Retarder. Lay-in cheeks with a small amount of Santa Red + Flesh Tone as shown. Use a mop to soften and blend.

4. Shade around nose, under eyebrows, behind eyelids, under chin, and under lips with Burnt Sienna as shown.

5. Highlight nose, above top lip, and above chin with Buttermilk as shown.

6. Base mouth with Santa Red + Flesh Tone as shown. Line mouth opening with Black Plum. Shade along bottom of top lip and along top of bottom lip with Cranberry Wine. Add sparkles on lips with Titanium White.

7. Base eyes with Buttermilk as shown. Add irises with Forest Green. Add pupils with Black "tornadoes." Add a sparkle to eyes with Titanium White. Shade across tops of eyes with Lamp Black.

8. Line eyelashes and eyebrows with Burnt Sienna as shown. Line across bottom of eyes with Burnt Sienna.

Detailing:

1. Float tops and bottoms of sleeves at wrists and top and bottom of neckline with Cranberry Wine. Line with Cranberry Wine.

2. Line around wrists and neck with Rich Gold. Drybrush with Pale Gold.

3. Add lace to sleeves and neck by making a triangular dotted design with Rich Gold.

Sash:

1. Base sash with two coats of Cranberry Wine. Shade with Black Plum. Highlight with Santa Red.

2. Line holly leaves and veins with Rich Gold. Refer to Brocade Vest and Trim Pattern on page 89.

Base:

1. Base top edge of base with Rich Gold. Base remaining area of base with Cranberry Wine. Shade top, below edge, with Black Plum.

2. Add lettering with Rich Gold.

3. Line holly leaves with Rich Gold.

4. Dot berries with Buttermilk. Wash over berries with Cranberry Wine.

Finish:

1. Using a hot-glue gun, glue wig in place. Tie hair back with a ribbon.

2. Assemble as shown in photo on page 84.

Princess' Face Pattern

3–7

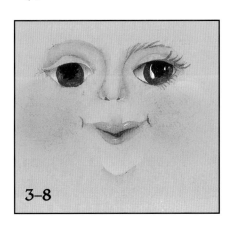

3–8

Nutcracker Prince—

Quilted Coat:

1. Base the coat with Buttermilk as shown.

2. Lightly mark quilting pattern on coat and sleeves with a pencil as shown.

3. Highlight top of quilting with Titanium White as shown. Shade bottom of quilting with Raw Sienna.

4. Using ¼"-wide tape, mask off ¼" away from edge of buttons, bottom of coat, and top edges of cuffs as shown. Base stripes with three or four coats of Cranberry Wine. Remove tape.

5. Line stripes with Pale Gold as shown.

6. Transfer Brocade Vest and Trim Pattern from below onto stripes.

7. Base holly leaves with Forest Green as shown. Line leaves and veins with Pale Gold. Add scrolls with Pale Gold.

8. Dot berries with Buttermilk as shown. Shade with Santa Red.

9. Base buttons with Rich Gold as shown. Shade under buttons with Raw Sienna.

10. Add one-strokes on buttons with Cranberry Wine as shown.

Epilets:

1. Base epilets with Pale Gold. Shade with Rich Gold.

2. Line holly leaves and veins on epilets with Cranberry Wine.

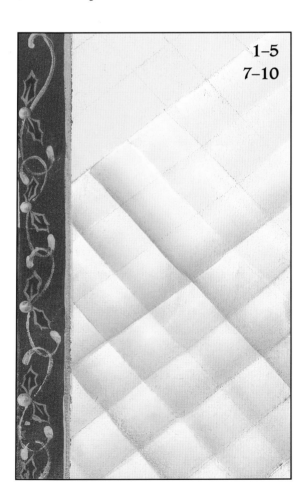

1–5
7–10

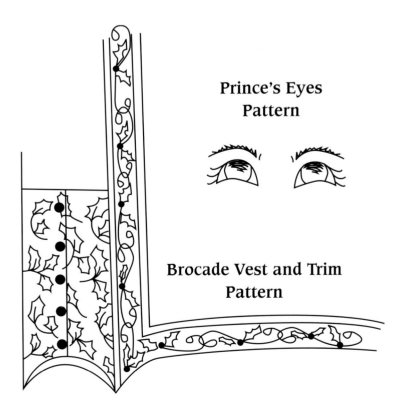

Prince's Eyes
Pattern

Brocade Vest and Trim
Pattern

Shirt Ruffles:

1. Highlight ruffles with Titanium White, ruffling paintbrush as you float. Shade under ruffles with Raw Sienna.

Vest:

1. Base vest with Buttermilk.

2. Transfer Brocade Vest and Trim Pattern from page 89 onto vest.

3. Line holly leaves and scrolls with Rich Gold. Dot buttons with Rich Gold. Line buttonholes with Raw Sienna.

4. Shade down center of vest and under coat with Raw Sienna. Highlight with Titanium White. Shade bottom of vest with Rich Gold.

Pants:

1. Base pants with Buttermilk. Dry-brush highlight down center with Titanium White.

2. Shade top and bottom of pants with Raw Sienna.

3. Base one ¹/₈"-wide stripe down each side of pants with Cranberry Wine. Add "S" strokes over stripes with Pale Gold.

Gloves:

1. Base gloves with Titanium White. Shade with Charcoal Grey + Titanium White.

Hat:

1. Base hat with Buttermilk. Dry-brush top of hat with Titanium White.

2. Transfer Crown Pattern from below onto hat.

3. Base crown and plume with Pale Gold. Shade around crown and bottom of hat with Raw Sienna.

4. Add reverse teardrops on crown with Raw Sienna.

Crown Pattern

Add dots above teardrops with Cranberry Wine. Highlight with Santa Red + Titanium White.

5. Base button below plume with Cranberry Wine. Add holly leaves and veins with Pale Gold. Shade bottom of button with Charcoal. Highlight top of button with Santa Red. Add comma-strokes on plume with Rich Gold.

6. Base hat brim with Charcoal Grey. Shade with Lamp Black. Add "S" strokes on brim with Pale Gold.

Face:

1. Base face with Flesh Tone.

2. Transfer Prince's Eyes Pattern from page 89 onto face.

3. Dry-brush cheeks with Santa Red + Flesh Tone.

4. Base eyes with Buttermilk. Add irises with Forest Green. Add pupils with Black "tornadoes." Add a sparkle to eyes with Titanium White. Shade across tops of eyes with Lamp Black.

5. Shade behind eyes, under hat, next to coat, under eyebrows, and under moustache with Burnt Sienna.

6. Highlight under eyes and above cheek with Buttermilk.

7. Base moustache with Raw Sienna. Shade moustache under nose with Lamp Black. Line several hairs with Raw Sienna + Buttermilk.

8. Line tops of eyes and eyebrows with Raw Sienna.

9. Base teeth with Buttermilk. Highlight with Titanium White. Line teeth with Charcoal Grey + Titanium White.

10. Base lips with Santa Red. Shade with Cranberry Wine. Highlight with Titanium White. Shade teeth under top lip with Charcoal Grey.

Sword:

1. Base sword with Pale Gold. Shade with Rich Gold.

2. Line holly leaves, veins, and scrolls with Rich Gold.

3. Dot a berry on handle with Cranberry Wine. Highlight with Santa Red + Titanium White.

4. Line insignia on bottom with Rich Gold.

Boots:

1. Base boots with Charcoal Grey. Shade with Lamp Black. Dry-brush highlight toes and centers of boots with Charcoal Grey + Titanium White.

2. Paint buttons with Rich Gold. Add one-strokes below buttons with Pale Gold.

Base:

1. Base top of base with Buttermilk.

2. Shade around boots with Raw Sienna.

3. Base routed edge with Pale Gold. Shade with Rich Gold.

4. Base holly leaves with Forest Green. Line leaves and veins with Pale Gold.

5. Dot berries with Buttermilk. Shade with Santa Red. Highlight with Pale Gold.

6. Line scrolls with Cranberry Wine.

7. Base bottom edge with Cranberry Wine.

8. Add lettering with Rich Gold.

Finish:

1. Using a hot-glue gun, glue hair in place. Glue beads along hat brim. Glue fringe around epilets. Glue braid trim over one arm.

2. Assemble as shown in photo on page 84.

92

CONTAINERS

Paint Palettes:

Accent:
Peaches-n-Cream

Deco Art:
Berry Red
Black Forest Green
Black Plum
Blue Mist
Boysenberry Pink
Bright Green
Burnt Orange
Burnt Sienna
Burnt Umber
Buttermilk
Charcoal Grey
Cranberry Wine
Dark Pine
Flesh Tone
Forest Green
French Mocha
Kelly Green
Lamp Black
Lavender
Marigold
Mint Julep Green
Mississippi Mud
Mistletoe
Moon Yellow
Olive Green
Payne's Grey
Raw Sienna
Royal Purple
Russet
Silver Sage Green
Taffy Cream
Tangerine
Titanium White
Toffee
True Red
Twinkles

Delta:
Maple Sugar

JoSonja:
Carbon Black
Norwegian Orange
Pearl White

Supplies:
Wooden Containers
Fantasy Snow (Delta)
Texture Paste (JoSonja)
Sparkle Découpage
Crystal Glitter
Gold Leaf Adhesive
Aluminum Leaf
Gold Leaf

Sticks Toothpick Holder—

Snowman:

1. Base snowman, inside and outside, with Blue Mist. Stipple with Blue Mist + Titanium White.

2. Stipple snowman with a light coat of Fantasy Snow. Let dry. Repeat.

3. Apply a heavy coat of Sparkle Découpage over Fantasy Snow. Let dry.

Face:

1. Using a palette knife, mix Texture Paste with Carbon Black (1:1) and fill a plastic sandwich bag.

2. Make a small cut at one corner of the bag. Squeeze two eyes and a mouth onto palette. Place a $1/4$" end of a toothpick into mouth. Let dry.

3. Mix Texture Paste with Norwegian Orange (1:1) and fill a plastic sandwich bag. Repeat Step 2 above for nose.

4. Highlight eyes with Pearl White. Add a comma-stroke on left sides of eyes and a dot in upper right corners of eyes with Pearl White.

5. Shade bottom of nose with Cranberry Wine. Highlight across top of nose with Pearl White.

6. Using a hot-glue gun, glue eyes, nose, and mouth onto face.

Hat:

1. Base hat with Cranberry Wine. Rake one direction with Berry Red. To create crosshatching, repeat in opposite direction. To create a woven pattern, rake one direction with Boysenberry Pink + Berry Red. Repeat in opposite direction.

2. Shade above and below hatband with Black Plum. Base hatband with Black Forest Green.

3. Base holly leaves around hatband with Dark Pine. Line leaves and veins with Kelly Green

+ Mint Julep Green. Dot berries with Berry Red. Highlight tops of berries with a small dot of Boysenberry Pink.

"Pepper Mint" Container—

Face, Hands, and Hair:

Note: Refer to Diagram A below.

1. Base face and hands with Peaches-n-Cream. Shade with Burnt Sienna.

2. Dry-brush cheeks and base nose with Peaches-n-Cream + True Red. Shade across top of nose with True Red.

3. Base eyes with Titanium White. Add irises with Forest Green. Add pupils with Lamp Black.

4. Line lips with True Red + a small amount of Peaches-n-Cream. Add highlights to pupils, nose, and lips with Titanium White.

5. Line eyebrows, moustache, and around eyes with Charcoal Grey.

6. Base hair with Charcoal Grey. Shade hair under hat with Lamp Black.

Hat and Pants:

1. Base hat and pants with Titanium White. Base stripes on hat and pants with True Red. Shade around top and bottom of hat and on pants with Payne's Grey.

2. Base fur areas on hat with Silver Sage Green. Stipple with Titanium White.

Shirt:

1. Base shirt with True Red. Shade under vest with Black Plum. Dry-brush highlight in center of sleeves with True Red + Moon Yellow. Shade sleeves with Black Plum.

Vest:

1. Base vest with Silver Sage Green. Shade around vest with Forest Green.

2. Transfer Candy Cane Pattern from below onto back of vest.

3. Base candy cane with Titanium White. Add stripes with True Red.

4. Add continuous "S" strokes around vest with Silver Sage Green.

Shoes and Belt:

1. Base shoes and belt with Forest Green. Shade shoes and belt with Black Forest Green. Dry-brush highlight tips of shoes with Silver Sage Green. Highlight top of belt with Silver Sage Green.

2. Base soles of shoes with Black Forest Green.

Belt Buckle and Peppermint Bowl:

1. Base belt buckle and peppermint candies with Titanium White. Add stripes with True Red. Shade with Payne's Grey. Add a thin highlight linc with Titanium White.

2. To create a "glass" bowl, float around bowl with Titanium White. Add shine marks on bowl with Titanium White.

Finish:

1. Glaze over hat, belt buckle, and peppermint candies with Pearl White.

2. Base inside of container with Forest Green.

Diagram A

Candy Cane Pattern

"Goody Gumdrop" Container—

Note: Refer to Diagram B on page 97.

Face, Hands, and Hair:

1. Base face and hands with Peaches-n-Cream. Shade with Burnt Sienna.

2. Base hair with Moon Yellow. From top down, rake in Moon Yellow + Burnt Sienna. From bottom up, rake in Taffy Cream.

3. Dry-brush cheeks with Peaches-n-Cream + Berry Red.

4. Base eyes with Titanium White. Add irises with Mistletoe. Add pupils with Lamp Black. Shade across tops of eyes with Lamp Black. Add a highlight dot to eyes with Titanium White. Line around eyes and eyelids with Burnt Sienna.

5. Line mouth with Berry Red. Float a narrow float across top of lips with Berry Red.

6. Line eyebrows and nose with Burnt Sienna. Reverse-float down center of eyelids with Titanium White.

Hat:

1. Base pom-pom on top of hat with Royal Purple.

2. Base center section of hat with Mistletoe. Shade with Black Forest Green.

3. Base brim with Berry Red.

Pants:

1. Base pants with Mistletoe. Using a #2 liner, line plaid pattern on pants with Titanium White. Shade top and bottom with Black Forest Green.

Belt and Belt Buckle:

1. Base belt with Boysenberry Pink. Shade top and bottom with Berry Red.

2. Base belt buckle with Taffy Cream. Shade around edge with Moon Yellow.

Shoes:

1. Base shoes with Royal Purple + Titanium White.

2. Base soles of shoes with Royal Purple + Titanium White (2:1). Shade above soles with Royal Purple. Dry-brush highlight across tops of shoes with Titanium White.

Sweater:

1. Base sweater with Mint Julep Green.

2. Stipple dark ribbing on collar, armbands, and around bottom of sweater with Mistletoe + Mint Julep Green. Stipple light ribbing with Mint Julep Green + Titanium White.

3. Shade around arms, neck, and below collar with Mistletoe. Darken with a Black Forest Green wash.

4. Alternately stipple gumdrops around sweater with Royal Purple + Titanium White, Boysenberry Pink, Taffy Cream, and Mistletoe.

Stipple-shade around bottoms of purple gumdrops with Royal Purple, pink gumdrops with Berry Red, yellow gumdrops with Moon Yellow, and green gumdrops with Black Forest Green.

5. Add knitting design on collar with Royal Purple, Mistletoe, Moon Yellow, and Berry Red.

Bowl of Gumdrops:

1. Stipple gumdrops as in Sweater, Step 4 above.

2. Aluminum-leaf bowl, following manufacturer's directions.

3. Shade bowl with Lamp Black.

Finish:

1. Apply a coat of Sparkle Découpage over hat, belt buckle, and gumdrops. Sprinkle with crystal glitter. Let dry.

2. Base inside of container with Mistletoe.

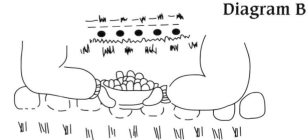

Diagram B

"Merry Marzipan" Container—

Note: Refer to Diagram C on page 98.

Face, Hands, and Hair:

1. Base headpiece with Peaches-n-Cream.

2. Base hair with Mississippi Mud. Shade on face around hair with Burnt Sienna. Rake in hair with Burnt, Umber, then again with Mississippi Mud + Toffee. Rake toward bun and shade behind bun with Burnt Umber. Rake in bangs with Burnt Umber.

3. Dry-brush cheeks with Peaches-n-Cream + Berry Red.

4. Base eyes with Titanium White. Add irises with Royal Purple. Add pupils with Lamp Black. Add a highlight dot to eyes with Titanium White. Shade across tops of eyes with Lamp Black.

5. Line eyelashes with Burnt Umber.

6. Highlight across bridge of nose with Buttermilk. Shade under nose with Burnt Sienna.

7. Line mouth with Berry Red + Peaches-n-Cream. Shade between lips and at corners of mouth with Berry Red + Cranberry Wine.

Hat and Dress:

1. Base hat and dress with Black Forest Green.

2. Highlight collar with Buttermilk. Randomly high-

light top of Buttermilk with Titanium White.

3. Wash apron with Buttermilk, leaving it streaky. Highlight with Titanium White.

4. Transfer Fruit Border Pattern from below onto apron.

5. Base pear with Moon Yellow. Shade with Raw Sienna. Base strawberry with Berry Red. Shade with Cranberry Wine. Base grapes with Lavender. Shade with Royal Purple. Base orange with Tangerine. Shade with Burnt Orange.

6. Base leaves with Mistletoe. Shade with Black Forest Green.

7. Highlight gathers on apron with Titanium White.

Note: You will need to "float" through some of the fruit.

8. Add dots to lace collar and around bottom of apron with Titanium White.

9. Base holly leaves with Mistletoe. Line leaves and veins with Pale Gold. Dot berries with Berry Red. Shade bottoms of berries with Cranberry Wine.

Hat:

1. Base pom-pom at top of hat with Lamp Black + Titanium White. Stipple with

Buttermilk, then again with Titanium White.

2. Base center section of hat with Black Forest Green.

3. Base brim with Cranberry Wine. Stipple with Berry Red, then again with Berry Red + Moon Yellow.

4. Transfer Fruit Pattern from below onto hat.

5. Dampen area with fruit with water. Wash pear with Raw Sienna, strawberry with Cranberry Wine, grapes with Royal Purple, and orange with Burnt Orange. Dry thoroughly. Repeat two or three times working more color into the right sides of the fruits.

6. Highlight upper right sides of pear with Marigold, strawberry with Berry Red, grapes with Lavender, and orange with Burnt Orange + Tangerine. Repeat until desired intensity is reached.

7. Further highlight pear with Moon Yellow, strawberry with Berry Red + Moon Yellow, grapes with Lavender + Titanium White, and orange with Tangerine.

8. Add final highlight on pear, grapes, and orange with Buttermilk and on strawberry with Moon Yellow.

9. Base grape leaves and strawberry calyx with Bright Green. Line pine sprigs with

Lamp Black, then again with Mistletoe, then again with Bright Green. Highlight with Olive Green.

10. Base holly leaves with Mistletoe. Line with Pale Gold. Dot berries with Berry Red.

11. Wash fruit on hat with Twinkles.

Belt and Belt Buckle:

1. Base belt with Cranberry Wine. Highlight top edge with Berry Red. Dry-brush highlight with Berry Red + Moon Yellow.

2. Base belt buckle with Pale Gold.

Finish:

1. Base inside of container with Black Forest Green.

Diagram C

Fruit Pattern

Fruit Border Pattern

"Frankie Fudge" Container—

Note: Refer to Diagram D on page 100.

Face and Hands:

1. Base face with Peaches-n-Cream. Shade around top of head, under hat, bottom of head, and above jacket and shirt with Burnt Sienna.

2. Shade around nose with Burnt Sienna. Highlight with Buttermilk.

3. Dry-brush cheeks with Peaches-n-Cream + True Red.

4. Line mouth with Peaches-n-Cream + True Red.

5. Base eyes with Buttermilk. Add irises with Mistletoe. Add pupils with Lamp Black. Line eyebrows with Burnt Sienna.

6. Add a stronger highlight to eyes, nose, cheeks, and mouth with Buttermilk.

Pants:

1. Base pants with Toffee. Dry-brush highlight with Buttermilk. Shade with Russet.

2. Add stripes on pants with Cranberry Wine. Dry-brush highlight with True Red.

Shoes:

1. Base shoes with Russet. Shade with Black Plum.

Dry-brush highlight across tops of shoes with Toffee.

Belt, Belt Buckle, and Hat:

1. Base belt, belt buckle, and hat with Black Plum. Dry-brush center of belt with French Mocha. Stipple brim and pom-pom on hat with French Mocha, then again with Flesh Tone, then again with Toffee.

Shirt:

1. Base shirt with Buttermilk. Shade under jacket with Russet. Line with Russet.

Jacket:

1. Base jacket with French Mocha. Highlight with Flesh Tone. Dry-brush highlight in center of sleeves with Flesh Tone. Shade with Russet. Darken some shadows with Black Plum.

2. Transfer Christmas Tree Pattern from below onto pockets and back of jacket.

3. Base trees with Forest Green. Highlight tree branches with Mistletoe.

4. Base deer with Russet. Stipple fur with French Mocha.

Finish:

1. Base inside of container with Black Plum.

2. Gold-leaf hat, buttons, and belt buckle, following manufacturer's directions.

3. Shade gold leaf on hat and belt buckle with Russet.

Finish Insides:

1. If desired, gold-leaf insides of containers, following manufacturer's directions.

2. Fill with your favorite small candies or treats.

Christmas Tree Pattern

Diagram D

Paint Palettes:

Deco Art:
Alizarin Crimson
Antique Gold
Bitter Sweet Chocolate
Black Forest Green
Black Plum
Blue Mist
Boysenberry Pink
Bright Green
Burnt Sienna
Burnt Umber
Buttermilk
Charcoal
Cranberry Wine
Dark Pine
Desert Sand
Desert Turquoise
Eggplant
Flesh Tone
Forest Green
French Mocha
Green Mist
Grey Sky
Kelly Green
Lamp Black
Light Cinnamon
Marigold
Mink Tan
Mint Julep Green
Moon Yellow
Navy Blue
Neutral Grey
Payne's Grey
Pearl Black
Raw Sienna
Sable Brown
Sachet Pink
Santa Red
Taffy Cream
Titanium White

Toffee
Twinkles

Delta:
Adriatic Blue
Candy Bar
Grape
Maple Sugar

JoSonja:
Magic Mix
Pale Gold
Pearl White
Rich Gold

Supplies:
Wooden Box,
    10" x 7" x 2½"
Wooden Blocks,
    2"-square (12)

Note: All shading and highlighting floats should be kept "washy" and "layered" for greater color intensity.

Note: Before beginning to paint blocks, place together, three down and four across, and wrap tape around outside to keep them from moving. After painting each scene, varnish and let dry. Place tape around each edge of each block on the side with the painted picture. This will help protect picture from paint "dripping" down when you are painting remaining sides of blocks.

Box:

1. Base box, inside and outside, with Lamp Black.

2. Transfer Stage Pattern from pages 104–105 onto top of lid.

3. Base peppermint sticks with Titanium White. Add stripes with Santa Red and Dark Pine. Shade both sides with Lamp Black. Add a stronger highlight down centers of peppermint sticks with Titanium White.

4. Base curtain with Black Plum keeping the color more intense near the folds. Highlight with Cranberry Wine, then again with Alizarin Crimson, then again with Santa Red, decreasing the coverage of highlight with each consecutive color. Wash over Santa Red areas with Alizarin Crimson.

5. The poinsettias are double-loaded strokes of various shades of red. Dot centers with Moon Yellow. The leaves are double-loaded strokes of Dark Pine and Bright Green. Add dots with Pearl White.

6. Base ribbons with Boysenberry Pink + Cranberry Wine. Line details with Titanium White.

7. To create curtain ties, add "S" strokes with Rich Gold.

8. Base gumdrops with Grape, Moon Yellow, and Dark Pine. Stipple gumdrops by adding Titanium White to the

Presenting The Nutcracker

102

base color two to three times, using less with each application. Shade between gumdrops with Lamp Black.

9. Paint girl peeking out from behind curtain as in Gingersnaps Scene, Steps 5–10 on pages 114–115. Wash over girl with Lamp Black + Glazing Medium (1:3) to tone down colors.

10. Wash center area for lettering with Pearl Black.

11. Base "Presenting" with Kelly Green. Highlight with Bright Green. Base "The Nutcracker" with Rich Gold. Line right sides of letters with Kelly Green. Highlight on Kelly Green with Bright Green.

12. Transfer Candy Border from page 105 onto sides of box.

13. Paint candy canes as with peppermint sticks in Box, Step 3 on page 101.

14. Base lollipops with Bright Green, Boysenberry Pink, Taffy Cream, and Grape + Sachet Pink. Base lollipop sticks with Grey Sky. Highlight down centers with Titanium White. Shade where they overlap with Lamp Black. On each lollipop, float a darker value $3/16$" away from based color: Bright Green with Kelly Green, Boysenberry Pink with Santa Red, Taffy Cream

with Moon Yellow, and Grape + Sachet Pink with Grape. Highlight inside based color with a "C" stroke: Bright Green with Mint Julep Green, Taffy Cream with White, and Boysenberry Pink and Grape with Sachet Pink.

15. Base sugar cookies with Toffee. Shade around outer edges with Sable Brown. Add frosting by connecting "S" strokes $1/4$" from outer edges of each cookie. Dot centers of cookies with Santa Red and Kelly Green. Let dry. Paint inside frosting marks with Twinkles.

16. Base green-colored frosted cookie with Kelly Green. Dry-brush highlight with Mint Julep Green.

17. Base cake wedge with Burnt Umber. Base frosting with Mint Julep Green. Shade with Kelly Green. Highlight with Titanium White. Stipple in center of each layer with Sable Brown. Base whipped cream on cake top with Titanium White. Shade with Grey Sky.

18. Base cupcake foil with Rich Gold. Dry-brush where creases in the foil would be with Pale Gold. Shade between Pale Gold with Burnt Sienna. Base cupcakes with Sachet Pink. Highlight with Titanium White. Shade with Boysenberry Pink. Base

cherry with Boysenberry Pink, then again with Alizarin Crimson. Highlight with Boysenberry Pink. Shade with Black Plum.

19. Base wrapped candy with Santa Red. To create the wrapping, float $1/8$" around candy with Pearl White.

20. Base various chocolate bonbons using Burnt Umber and Sable Brown.

21. Base gumdrops and jelly beans as desired with various colors as desired.

Face Details (for all Nutcracker characters):

1. Base faces with Flesh Tone. Shade around hair with Burnt Sienna.

2. Dampen cheeks with Retarder. Lay-in cheeks with Alizarin Crimson + Flesh Tone. Use a mop to soften and blend.

3. Line mouths with Alizarin Crimson + Flesh Tone.

4. Base eyes with Buttermilk. Add irises according to individual instructions. Add pupils with Lamp Black. Shade across tops of eyes with Lamp Black. Line with Burnt Sienna. Shade under eyebrows with Burnt Sienna.

5. Highlight nose and chin with Buttermilk.

Stage Pattern

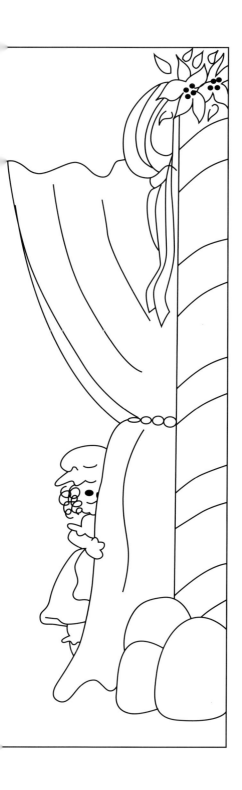

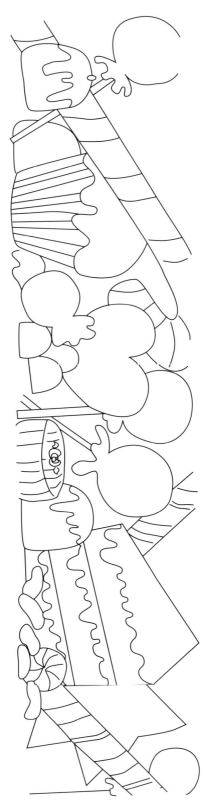

Candy Border Pattern

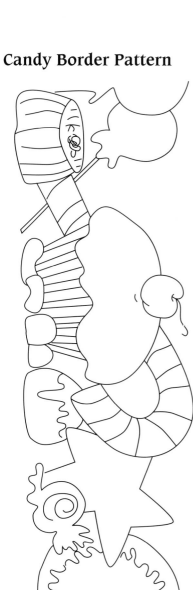

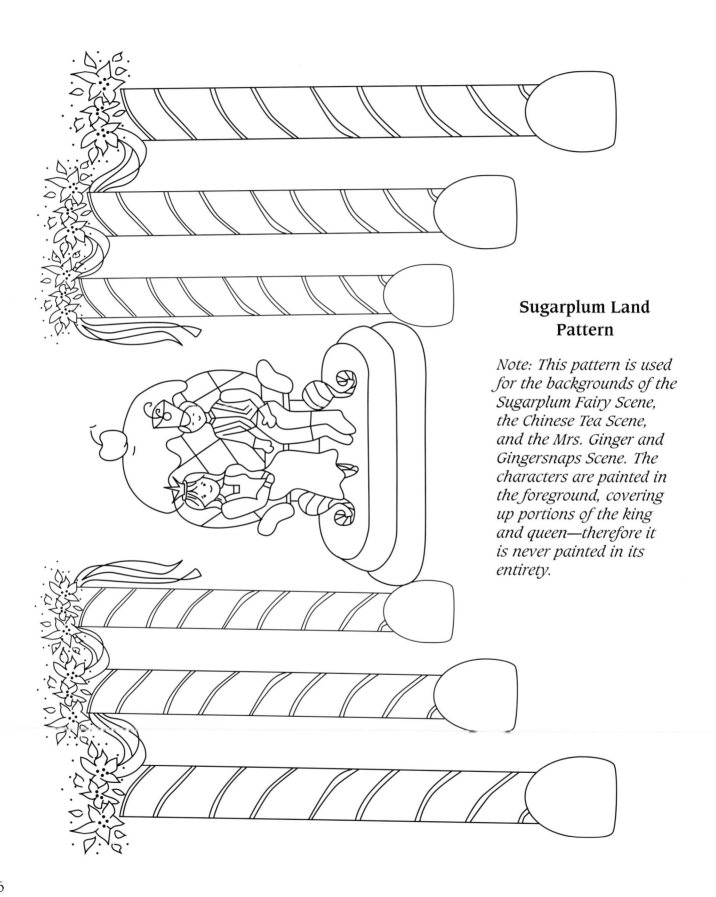

Sugarplum Land Pattern

Note: This pattern is used for the backgrounds of the Sugarplum Fairy Scene, the Chinese Tea Scene, and the Mrs. Ginger and Gingersnaps Scene. The characters are painted in the foreground, covering up portions of the king and queen—therefore it is never painted in its entirety.

Sugarplum Land:

1. Base background with Grey Sky + Adriatic Blue.

2. Transfer Sugarplum Land Pattern from page 106 onto blocks.

3. Base peppermint sticks with Titanium White. Add stripes with Santa Red and Kelly Green. Shade both sides with Payne's Grey. Add a stronger highlight down centers of peppermint sticks with Titanium White.

4. The poinsettias are double-loaded strokes of various shades of red and pink. Dot centers with Moon Yellow. The leaves are double-loaded strokes of Bright Green and Black Forest Green. Add dots with Pearl White.

5. Base ribbons with Sachet Pink. Shade with Boysenberry Pink. Line details with Titanium White.

6. Base gumdrops with Grape, Moon Yellow, and Kelly Green. Stipple purple gumdrops with Grape + Sachet Pink, then again with Sachet Pink, then again with Titanium White. Stipple yellow gumdrops with Buttermilk, then again with Titanium White. Stipple green gumdrops with Mint Julep Green, then again with Mint Julep Green + Titanium White.

Shade beneath gumdrops with Payne's Grey.

7. Base whipped cream on throne with Titanium White. Shade with Payne's Grey. Base cherry with Boysenberry Pink. Shade with Santa Red. Line stem with Santa Red.

8. Base back of throne with Mint Julep Green. Highlight with Titanium White. Shade with Kelly Green. Add a dot in center of each "diamond" with Boysenberry Pink.

9. Base "jelly bean" arm rests with Grape. Dry-brush highlight down centers with Sachet Pink. Add a stronger highlight with Titanium White.

10. Base throne legs with Titanium White. Add stripes with Santa Red. Shade with Payne's Grey.

11. Base "custard" steps with Buttermilk. Shade with French Mocha. Highlight with Titanium White.

12. Paint Princess Clara and The Nutcracker Prince as in Nutcracker Royalty: Princess Clara on pages 85–87 and Nutcracker Prince on pages 89–91.

Note: Disregard intricate detailing.

13. Wash between background peppermint sticks and over throne with Magic Mix + Titanium White.

14. Shade beneath throne with Payne's Grey.

Snow Queen Scene:

1. Slip-slap background with Adriatic Blue, Grey Sky, and Buttermilk.

Note: Keep it darker in sky area and lighter in ground area.

2. Transfer trees from Snow Queen Pattern on page 109 onto blocks.

3. Using a double-loaded paintbrush, slip-slap upper $^2/_3$ of each layer of branches with Green Mist and Forest Green.

4. The lower $^1/_3$ is slip-slapped with Titanium White.

Note: Work up into green areas with a dry paintbrush. You may need to repeat Step 4 two or three times until desired density is achieved.

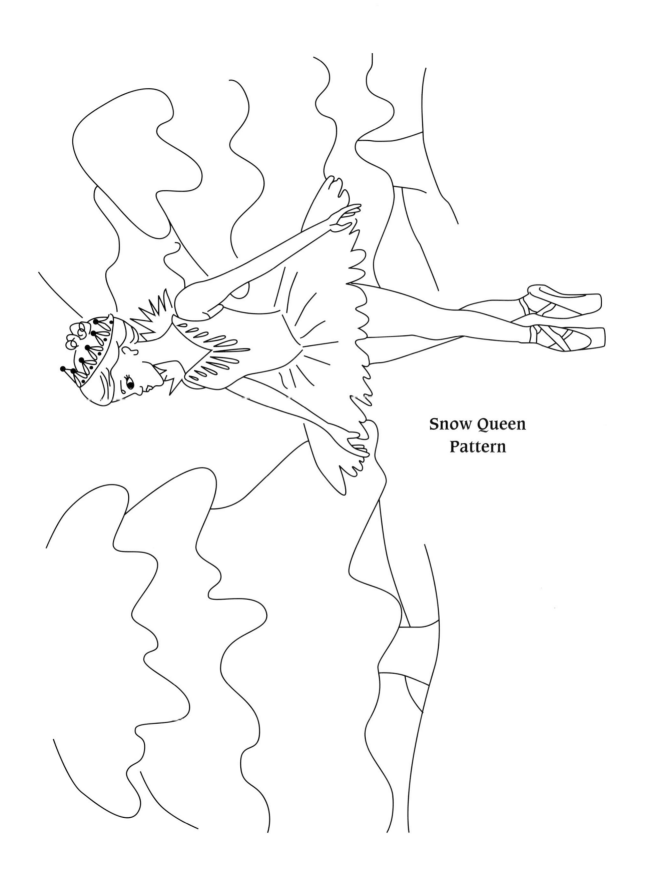

Snow Queen
Pattern

5. Wash over background tree with Adriatic Blue. Wash over foreground trees with Titanium White. Shade shadows on trees with Adriatic Blue. Wash trunks with Sable Brown. Shade with Adriatic Blue.

6. Highlight background snow mounds with Grey Sky. Highlight foreground snow mounds with Titanium White.

7. Splatter background with Titanium White.

8. Transfer dancer from Snow Queen Pattern onto blocks.

9. Paint face details as in Face Details, Steps 1–5 on page 103. Add iris with Candy Bar. Add small comma strokes for eyebrow with Burnt Sienna.

10. Base neck, arms, and legs with Flesh Tone. Highlight with Buttermilk. Add a stronger highlight with Titanium White. Shade with Burnt Sienna. Line details on skin areas with Burnt Sienna.

11. Base hair with Candy Bar. Line hair with Burnt Sienna, then again with Sable Brown.

12. Base connected teardrops on crown with Pearl White. Line details with Twinkles.

13. Add a few complete snowflakes near queen with Titanium White, then again with Pearl White.

14. Base tutu and toe shoes with Blue Mist. Rake tutu skirt with Titanium White. Wash tutu and toe shoes with Pearl White. Shade tutu with Blue Mist. Darken shadows with Desert Turquoise. Using the hit/skip method, work around tutu with Desert Turquoise.

Sugarplum Fairy Scene:

1. Paint background as in Sugarplum Land, Steps 1–14 on page 107.

2. Transfer Sugarplum Fairy Pattern from below onto blocks.

3. Paint face details as in Face Details, Steps 1–5 on page 103. Add irises with Adriatic Blue. Add small comma-strokes for eyebrows with Burnt Sienna.

Sugarplum Fairy Pattern

4. Base neck, arms, and legs with Flesh Tone. Highlight with Buttermilk. Shade with Burnt Sienna. Line details on skin areas with Burnt Sienna.

5. Base hair with Burnt Umber. Shade with Lamp Black. Highlight with Light Cinnamon.

6. Base crown and wand with Eggplant + Pearl White. Line details with Eggplant.

7. Base tutu skirt with Eggplant. Rake tutu skirt with Pearl White. Add some shadows back in with Eggplant + Pearl White. Base bodice and toe shoes with Eggplant + Pearl White. Shade with Eggplant. Line details on bodice with Pearl White. Line bottom of tutu skirt with an irregular line of Eggplant.

Chinese Tea Scene:

1. Paint background as in Sugarplum Land, Steps 1–14 on page 107.

2. Transfer Chinese Tea Pattern from page 113 onto blocks.

3. Paint face details as in Face Details, Steps 1–5 on page 103. Add irises with Burnt Umber.

4. Base hair with Lamp Black. Dry-brush highlight with Neutral Grey.

5. Base hats with Raw Sienna. Rake strokes with Moon Yellow, first vertically, then horizontally following contours of hats. Wash with Pale Gold. Line tassels with Boysenberry Pink, Adriatic Blue, and Alizarin Crimson.

6. Base shirts with Lamp Black. Create swirls with Adriatic Blue and Kelly Green as shown on page 113. Base stylized tulips with Boysenberry Pink + Alizarin Crimson.

Chinese Tea Pattern

Line details with Pale Gold. Shade with Lamp Black. Highlight with Neutral Grey.

7. Line details around sleeves, pants, and down fronts of shirts with Rich Gold.

8. Base pants, fans, inside sleeves, inside shirt, and inside hat on background dancers with Boysenberry Pink. Wash over all areas with Alizarin Crimson + Pearl White, except on fans and side of shirt. Shade with Alizarin Crimson. Highlight knees with Pearl White.

9. Base pants, under hat, and inside sleeves on foreground dancer with Cranberry Wine. Wash over all areas with Alizarin Crimson + Pearl White. Shade with Alizarin Crimson. Highlight knees with Pearl White.

10. Base fans with Pearl White. Highlight tops with Sachet Pink.

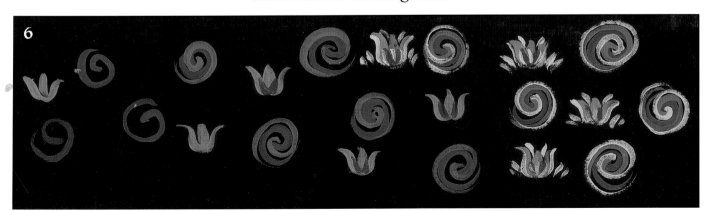

6

Mrs. Ginger and Gingersnaps Scene:

1. Paint background as in Sugarplum Land, Steps 1–14 on page 107.

2. Transfer Gingersnaps Pattern from page 115 onto blocks.

3. Paint face details as in Face Details, Steps 1–5 on page 103. Add irises with Kelly Green.

4. Base Mrs. Ginger's hair with Candy Bar. Shade with Lamp Black. Highlight with Marigold. Base hair ribbon with Sachet Pink + Boysenberry Pink.

5. Base Mrs. Ginger's skirt with Moon Yellow. Base under skirt with Marigold. Wash over skirt with Magic Mix + Pearl White.

6. Base Mrs. Ginger's apron, blouse, pantaloons, and bodice with Buttermilk. Shade apron, blouse, and pantaloons with Marigold. Highlight with Titanium White. To create lace edging, add irregular dots around collar and bottom of apron with Titanium White. Add stripes on bodice with Boysenberry Pink, Cranberry Wine, and Marigold. Shade bodice with Cranberry Wine. Line lacing on bodice with Charcoal.

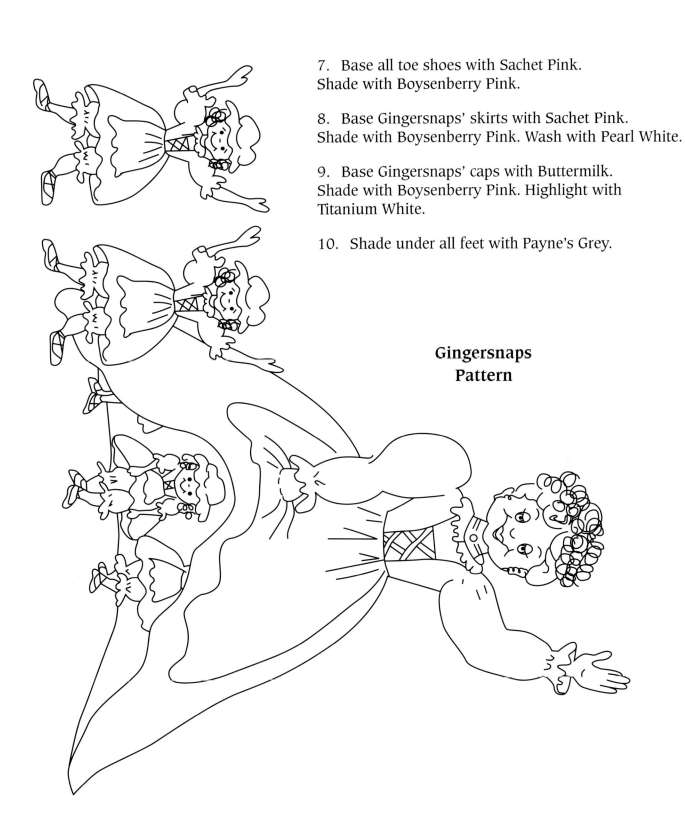

7. Base all toe shoes with Sachet Pink. Shade with Boysenberry Pink.

8. Base Gingersnaps' skirts with Sachet Pink. Shade with Boysenberry Pink. Wash with Pearl White.

9. Base Gingersnaps' caps with Buttermilk. Shade with Boysenberry Pink. Highlight with Titanium White.

10. Shade under all feet with Payne's Grey.

**Gingersnaps
Pattern**

115

Sleigh Ride Scene:

1. Paint background as in Snow Queen Scene, Steps 1–7 on pages 108–110.

2. Transfer Sleigh Ride Pattern from page 118 onto blocks.

3. Base reindeer legs, hind quarters, belly, and head with Light Cinnamon. Base neck and upper back with Sable Brown.

4. Over the Light Cinnamon areas, rake in areas marked in Diagram A on page 117 with Lamp Black making certain to follow the same direction so fur lays properly.

Note: Use a #8 pure sable round paintbrush loaded with "inky" consistency paint.

Flatten the bristles out by laying the paintbrush perpendicular to your palette. This will resemble a rake brush, but you will have more control and the paint will flow better.

5. Rake over and on either side of these areas with Bitter Sweet Chocolate. Rake outside these areas with Antique Gold. Add a final highlight with Maple Sugar.

6. Wash over these areas with Light Cinnamon. Rake over Sable Brown areas with Bitter Sweet Chocolate. Rake on either side of these areas with Mink Tan, then again with Desert Sand. Add a final highlight with Buttermilk.

7. Shade down backs of legs, under cheeks on necks, between ears, between reindeer, and under tails with Bitter Sweet Chocolate.

8. Base eyes with Lamp Black. Add "C" strokes for pupils with Light Cinnamon. Add a highlight to eyes with Buttermilk.

9. Base noses and hooves with Lamp Black. Highlight with Neutral Grey. Highlight noses with Desert Sand.

10. Base antlers with Sable Brown. Dry-brush highlight "tips" with Buttermilk. Dry-brush with Burnt Umber.

11. Base harness with Black Forest Green. Add strokework with Pale Gold. Line details with Alizarin Crimson. Dot between strokes with Santa Red. Add reins with Lamp Black. Dry-brush highlight with Neutral Grey.

12. Base sleigh with Boysenberry Pink. Base with two coats of Alizarin Crimson. Shade with Black Plum. Base negative areas inside sleigh with Black Plum. Add details with Pale Gold.

13. Base blanket with Forest Green. Apply a thin layer of Retarder over blanket, then base with Black Forest Green. Using a crumpled piece of plastic wrap, pounce over areas. Let dry. Highlight with Bright Green. Shade with Black Forest Green. Add details with Pale Gold.

14. Paint Princess Clara as in Nutcracker Royalty: Princess Clara on pages 85–87. Base cape with Boysenberry Pink. Shade with Cranberry Wine. Highlight with Sachet Pink. Base fur with Charcoal + Buttermilk. Stipple with Buttermilk, then again with Titanium White.

Note: Disregard intricate detailing.

15. Paint The Nutcracker Prince as in Nutcracker Royalty: Nutcracker Prince on pages 89–91. Base cape with Cranberry Wine. Highlight with Santa Red. Shade with Black Plum. Base ermine with Buttermilk. Line marks with Charcoal.

Note: Disregard intricate detailing.

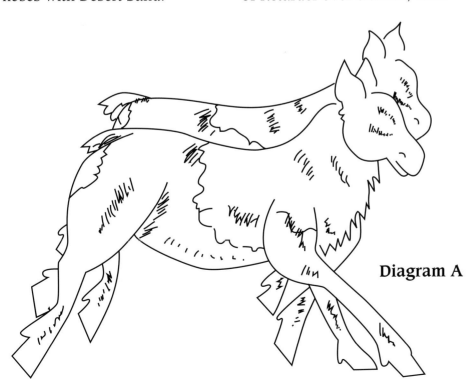

Diagram A

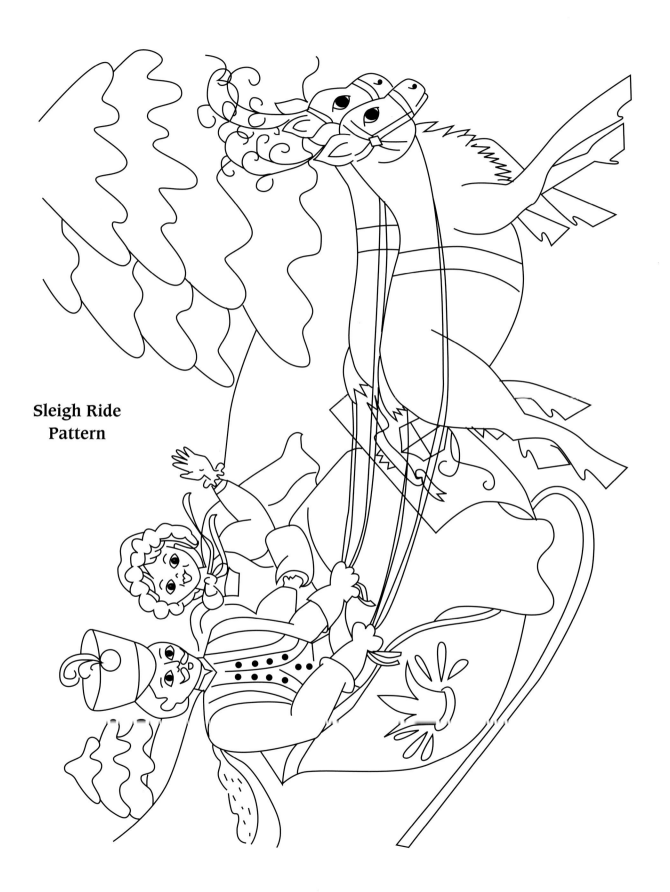

Sleigh Ride
Pattern

118

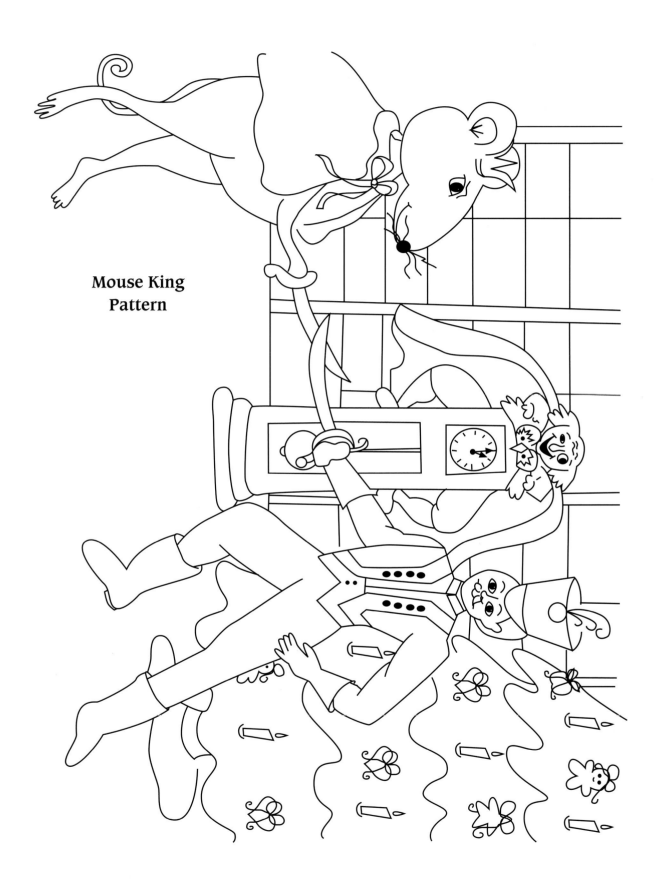

Mouse King
Pattern

119

Mouse King Scene:

1. Transfer Mouse King Pattern from page 119 onto blocks.

2. Base window with Navy Blue. Splatter with Titanium White.

3. Base wainscoting below window with Grey Sky. Base walls to either side of window with Adriatic Blue + Grey Sky.

4. Base floor with Adriatic Blue.

5. Shade around wainscoting and window with Payne's Grey. Line window panes with Grey Sky. Highlight down centers with Buttermilk.

6. Base tree with Dark Pine. Ruffle-float highlight edges of limbs with Bright Green. Shade under limbs with Black Forest Green.

7. Base candlesticks with Boysenberry Pink. Base over candlesticks with Alizarin Crimson. Highlight with Boysenberry Pink. Shade at base of candles with Black Plum.

8. Base candle cups with Pale Gold. Add flames with double-loaded one-strokes loaded with Moon Yellow and Alizarin Crimson. Dry-brush a halo around each flame with Pale Gold.

9. Base cookies with Toffee. Shade around cookies with Sable Brown.

10. Dot eyes with Burnt Umber.

11. Base sugarplums with Eggplant. Base leaves with Pale Gold. Line veins with Rich Gold.

12. Base ribbons on decorations with Boysenberry Pink and Eggplant.

13. Base tree trunk with Sable Brown. Shade with Burnt Umber.

14. Base tree skirt with Boysenberry Pink, then again with Alizarin Crimson. Shade with Black Plum. Highlight with Boysenberry Pink.

15. Shade under tree and across top of four blocks with Payne's Grey.

16. Base Godfather's cape, arms, pants, and shoes with Lamp Black. Highlight with Eggplant + Titanium White. Base inside cape with Eggplant. Shade with Lamp Black.

17. Paint face details as in Face Details, Steps 1–5 on page 103. Add irises with Lamp Black.

18. Line mouth with Lamp Black.

19. Base Godfather's hair with Neutral Grey. Highlight with Titanium White.

20. Base stockings with Buttermilk. Shade with Sable Brown. Highlight with Titanium White.

21. Base clock with Sable Brown. Shade with Burnt Umber. Highlight with Toffee. Base inside clock with Blue Mist. Shade around outer edge with Adriatic Blue.

22. Base clock face with Buttermilk. Shade around face with Sable Brown. Add details with Rich Gold.

23. Base pendulum with Pale Gold. Shade with Rich Gold. Highlight with Pearl White.

24. Add streaks to make clock face and pendulum look like they are behind glass with Titanium White.

25. Add a few streaks to window panes with Titanium White.

26. Base mouse with Neutral Grey. Stipple with Neutral Grey + Buttermilk, then again with Buttermilk.

27. Add a stronger highlight on cheek, upper nose area, belly, and front thigh with Titanium White.

28. Base ear with Buttermilk. Shade inside ear with Sachet Pink.

29. Wash over cheek with Sachet Pink.

30. Base crown with Rich Gold. Shade with Burnt Sienna.

31. Base nose, hand, legs, and tail with Sachet Pink. Shade with French Mocha. Highlight with Buttermilk.

32. Base cape with Boysenberry Pink, then again with Alizarin Crimson. Highlight with Boysenberry Pink. Shade with Black Plum.

33. Base ermine with Buttermilk. Shade with Raw Sienna. Highlight with Titanium White.

34. Line "dashes" with Lamp Black.

35. Add details on cape with Rich Gold.

36. Base eye with Buttermilk. Add iris with Lamp Black. Add a highlight with Titanium White. Shade above and across top of eye with Lamp Black.

37. Paint The Nutcracker Prince as in Nutcracker Royalty: Nutcracker Prince on pages 89–91.

Note: Disregard intricate detailing.

38. Base swords with Pale Gold. Shade with Burnt Sienna, then again with Rich Gold.

39. Anchor feet and clock to floor with Payne's Grey.

MESSAGES FROM THE AUTHORS

In 1975, five friends and I were looking for a way to "renew" our-selves for a few hours each week. All together we had over 20 children and the responsibilities of home and family were taking its toll. With the support and encouragement of our husbands, we began to paint together one night a week. I knew from the first moment I picked up a paintbrush that I had found something that would bring me great satisfaction. After that first class, when my husband told me that my daisy and strawberry looked nice—and I didn't have to tell him "what" they were—I knew I was hooked. Twenty-seven years later, as I look back at all that I've been able to see and do because of my painting, I still realize that the most important thing that I have gained is the people. My old painting buddies, students that have come and gone, and the forever friends that I still paint with now—in class, at conventions, and in my local chapter, the Utah Guild of Heritage Artists—will still be with me when my hand begins to shake and my eyes won't focus and I won't be able to remember which end of the brush to use. My love and thanks to Leslie, Bonnie, Liz, Carol, and Connie for being there when the journey began. I love you all.   —*Kristen*

Kristen Birkeland, CDA

Heidi Fassmann, CDA

In 1986, I started my painting career through a community education class in Provo, Utah. In this class, I discovered my love for painting. Since that time, I have taken many classes and seminars by a variety of artists including Cheri Rol, Eleonore Zimmerman, and Gayle Oram. Kristen Birkeland has been my teacher, friend, and mentor these past 12 years. The most important lesson I have learned from these instructors is that anyone can learn to paint if there is a desire. For some of us, it just takes a little more practice than others. My best cheering section is my family. They are always anxiously awaiting my next project. It is a Christmas tradition to paint each one of my four children a Christmas ornament every year for the tree. I believe Christmas and painting are the beginning of lasting Christmas traditions. Finally, thanks to Glenn who has supported and encouraged me in my painting endeavors.   —*Heidi*

ACKNOWLEDGMENTS

We would like to thank Craig Zimmerman and Zim's, Inc., of Salt Lake City, Utah, for providing many of the surfaces that were used in this book and for presenting us with this opportunity to share our love of decorative painting with you.

Paintbrushes:

The majority of paintbrushes used in this book are Black Gold by FM® Brushes. The paintbrush recommended and used for making reverse teardrops is the Raphael Kolinsky® Quill #3.

Wood Sources:

Clair Mattas
408 East 1st Avenue
Hutchinson, KS 67501
(316) 665-6634 after 6 pm

- Tissue Box

Robinson's Woods
1057 Trumbull Avenue
Girard, OH 44420
216-759-3843

- Clock

Wayne's Woodenware, Inc.
1913 County Road II
Neenah, WI 54956
1-800-840-1497

- Match Holder

Zim's, Inc.
4370 South 300 West
Salt Lake City, UT 84107
1-800-453-6420
www.zimcrafts.com

- Blocks
- Box
- Memory Book
- Music Box

- Nativity Set
- Nutcrackers
- Plate
- Santa/Elf Containers
- Sleds/Sleighs
- Smokers
- Victorian Ornaments

PAINT CONVERSION CHARTS

Delta:	DecoArt:	Plaid:
Adriatic Blue	Blueberry + Lamp Black	Slate Blue
Apple Green	Yellow Green	Lime Yellow
Bittersweet	Tangerine	Tangerine
Black Cherry	Napa Red	Burgundy
Black Green	Black Green	Wrought Iron
Black	Lamp Black	Licorice
Blue Spruce	Antique Teal	Wintergreen
Blue Storm	Payne's Grey	Heartland Blue
Burnt Sienna	Terra Cotta + Burnt Orange	Burnt Sienna
Burnt Umber	Dark Chocolate	Burnt Umber
Butter Yellow	Moon Yellow	Buttercup
Cadet Blue	Deep Midnite Blue	Heartland Blue + touch of White
Candy Bar	Rookwood	Raspberry Wine + Burnt Umber
Chamomile		
Charcoal	Graphite	Wrought Iron
Chocolate Cherry	Black Plum	Dioxazine Purple +Burnt Umber
Cinnamon	Rookwood	Huckleberry
Dark Brown	Dark Chocolate	Maple Syrup
Dark Burnt Umber	Raw Umber	Dark Grey
Dark Flesh	Burnt Orange + Sable Brown	Buckskin Brown
Dark Jungle	Avocado + Burnt Umber	Green Meadow
Dark Forest Green	Plantation Pine	Thicket
Deep River	Hauser Dark Green	Hunter Green
Drizzle Grey	Grey Sky	Dove Grey
Empire Gold	Marigold	Turners Yellow
Flesh Tan	Sand	Taffy + Camel
Forest Green	Avocado	Old Ivy
Fruit Punch	Cadmium Red	Christmas Red
Grape	Plum	Plum Pudding
Green Sea	Green Mist	Poetry Green
Hippo Grey	Neutral Grey	Charcoal Grey + Dapple Grey
Ivory	Taffy Cream + White Taffy	
Leaf Green	Hauser Light Green	Fresh Foliage
Leprechaun	Arbor Green	Poetry Green
Liberty Blue	Sapphire	Thunder Blue + White
Light Ivory	Light Buttermilk	French Vanilla
Maple Sugar	Antique Gold + White	Buttercrunch
Medium Flesh	Mocha	Skintone
Metallic Bronze	Glorious Gold + Bronze Metallic	Solid Bronze Metallic
Metallic Gold	Glorious Gold Metallic	Antique Gold Metallic
Midnight Blue	Payne's Grey	Payne's Grey
Moroccan Red	Country Red	Calico Red
Mudstone	Slate Gray + Antique Gold	Barn Wood
Napthol Crimson	Brilliant Red	Lipstick Red
Old Parchment	Moon Yellow + White Sunflower	
Orange	Cadmium Orange	Red Light
Pale Gold	Venetian Gold Metallic	Champagne Metallic

Palomino	Sable Brown + Olive Green	Camel + Honey
Pearl Finish	White Pearl	Pearl White Metallic
Pearl Luster		
Persimmon	Blush + Cool Neutral	Poppy Red
Pine Green	Evergreen	Thicket
Quaker Grey	Grey Sky	Dove Grey
Rain Grey	Blue Grey	Mist White + Pure Black
Raspberry	Boysenberry	Hot Pink
Raw Sienna	Terra Cotta	Raw Sienna
Red Iron Oxide	Georgia Clay	Light Red Oxide
Rouge Blush	Flesh	Christmas Red + Peach Perfection
Sandstone	Antique White	Clay Bisque
Seminole	Hauser Medium	Green Clover
Spice Brown	Milk Chocolate	Nutmeg
Spice Tan	Antique Gold + Sable Brown	Honeycomb
Storm Grey	Graphite	Ivory Black + White
Terra Cotta	Terra Cotta + Oxblood	Terra Cotta
Territorial Beige	Sable Brown	Honeycomb
Tide Pool Blue	French Grey Blue + White	Porcelain Blue
Tomato Spice	Crimson Tide	Barnyard Red
Trail	Khaki Tan	Butter Pecan
Tuscan Red		
Victorian Teal		
Wedgewood Green	Jade Green	Bayberry
White	Titanium White	Titanium White

DecoArt:	**Delta:**	**Plaid:**
Alizarin Crimson	Black Cherry	Burgundy
Antique Gold	Antique Gold + Raw Sienna	Teddy Bear Tan
Asphaltum	Walnut	Raw Umber
Berry Red	Napthol Crimson	Crimson
Bitter Sweet Chocolate	Dark Burnt Umber	Burnt Umber
Black		
Black Forest Green	Deep River	Hunter Green
Black Green	Black Green	Wrought Iron
Black Plum	Chocolate Cherry	Dioxazine Purple + Burnt Umber
Blue Mist	Blue Wisp	Summer Sky
Boysenberry Pink	Fuchsia	Hot Pink
Bright Green	Jubilee Green	Evergreen
Burnt Orange	Georgia Clay	Terra Cotta
Burnt Sienna	Candy Bar	Rasberry Wine + Burnt Umber
Burnt Umber	Burnt Umber	Burnt Umber
Buttermilk	Antique White	Tapioca
Cadmium Red	Fruit Punch	Christmas Red
Charcoal Grey	Charcoal + Burnt Umber	Dark Grey + Black
Cranberry Wine	Mendocino + Burnt Umber	Raspberry Wine
Dark Pine	Hunter Green	Emerald Isle + Tart Green
Desert Sand	Sandstone	Clay Bisque
Desert Turquoise	Colonial Blue	Aqua + Cerulean Blue
Eggplant		
Emperor's Gold	Bronze Metallic + 14K Gold Metallic	Inca Gold Metallic + Solid Bronze Metallic
Evergreen	Forest Green	Thicket

Flesh Tone	Dunes	Skintone
Forest Green	Deep River	Shamrock
French Mocha	Santa Fe Rose	Huckleberry + White
Graphite	Charcoal	Ivory Black
Green Mist	Oasis Green	Poetry Green
Grey Sky	White + Bridgeport	Dove Grey
Kelly Green	Jubilee Green	Evergreen
Lamp Black	Black	Licorice
Lavender	Purple + White	Dioxazine Purple + Licorice
Light Cinnamon	Autumn Brown	Nutmeg
Light Hauser Green	Light Foliage Green	Light Hauser Green
Marigold	Empire Gold	Turners Yellow
Metallic Black Pearl	Black + Silver Metallic	Sequin Black Metallic
Metallic Silver		
Midnight Blue	Maganese Blue	Prussian Blue
Mink Tan	Light Chocolate	Nutmeg + White
Mint Julep Green	Christmas Green + White	Shamrock + White
Mississippi Mud	Burnt Umber + Cadet Grey	Burnt Umber +White
Mistletoe	Kelly Green	Evergreen
Moon Yellow	Old Parchment	Sunflower
Napa Red	Mulberry	Burgundy
Navy Blue	Prussian Blue	Prussian Blue
Neutral Grey	Hippo Grey	Medium Grey
Olive Green	Leaf Green + White	Fresh Foliage + White
Payne's Grey	Midnight Blue	Payne's Grey
Pearl Black	Black + Silver Metallic	Sequin Black Metallic
Raw Sienna	Raw Sienna	English Mustard Seed
Royal Purple	Vintage Wine	Dioxazine Purple + Licorice
Russet	Candy Bar	Huckleberry
Sable Brown	Territorial Beige	Nutmeg + Teddy Bear Tan
Sachet Pink		
Santa Red	Tompte Red	Napthol Crimson
Sapphire	Liberty Blue	Blue Ribbon
Silver Sage Green	Silver Pine White + Green Umber	
Taffy Cream	Pale Yellow	Lemonade
Tangerine	Bittersweet	Tangerine
Titanium White	White	Titanium White
Toffee	AC Flesh	Almond Parfait
Tomato Red	Cardinal Red	Calico Red
True Red	Fire Red	Cardinal Red
Twinkles		
Wedgewood Blue	Maganese Blue + Midnight	Thunder Blue

JoSonja:	**DecoArt:**	**Delta:**	**Plaid:**
Cadmium Scarlet	Cadmium Orange + Cadmium Red	Crimson	Red Light
Carbon Black	Lamp Black	Black	Licorice
Magic Mix			
Norwegian Orange	Delane's Cheek Color	Georgia Clay + Napthol Red Light	
Pale Gold	Glorious Gold Metallic	14K Gold Metallic	Pure Gold Metallic
Pearl White	White Pearl	Pearl Finish	Pearl White Metallic
Rich Gold	Venetian Gold Metallic	Kim Gold Metallic	Pure Gold Metallic

METRIC CONVERSION CHART

INCHES TO MILLIMETRES AND CENTIMETRES

MM-Millimetres   CM-Centimetres

INCHES	MM	CM	INCHES	CM	INCHES	CM
1/8	3	0.9	9	22.9	30	76.2
1/4	6	0.6	10	25.4	31	78.7
3/8	10	1.0	11	27.9	32	81.3
1/2	13	1.3	12	30.5	33	83.8
5/8	16	1.6	13	33.0	34	86.4
3/4	19	1.9	14	35.6	35	88.9
7/8	22	2.2	15	38.1	36	91.4
1	25	2.5	16	40.6	37	94.0
1 1/4	32	3.2	17	43.2	38	96.5
1 1/2	38	3.8	18	45.7	39	99.1
1 3/4	44	4.4	19	48.3	40	101.6
2	51	5.1	20	50.8	41	104.1
2 1/2	64	6.4	21	53.3	42	106.7
3	76	7.6	22	55.9	43	109.2
3 1/2	89	8.9	23	58.4	44	111.8
4	102	10.2	24	61.0	45	114.3
4 1/2	114	11.4	25	63.5	46	116.8
5	127	12.7	26	66.0	47	119.4
6	152	15.2	27	68.6	48	121.9
7	178	17.8	28	71.1	49	124.5
8	203	20.3	29	73.7	50	127.0

INDEX

MERRY CHRISTMAS GOD JUL

MERI KURISUMASU

JOYEUX NOEL

FELIZ NAVIDAD

BUON NATALE

WEIHNACHTEN

FROHE

NOLLIG SHONA

MELE KALIKIMAKA

VROLIJK KERSTFEEST